COMPLETE PRICE GUIDE TO ANTIQUE JEWELRY

COMPLETE PRICE GUIDE TO ANTIQUE JEWELRY

RICHARD E. GILBERT
JAMES H. WOLF

FIRST EDITION
ASHLAND PUBLICATIONS : SARASOTA FLORIDA

SPECIAL NOTICE

The information presented in this book, including values listed, have been compiled from the most reliable sources. Every possible effort has been made to eliminate errors and questionable information. The Publisher and/or Authors will not be held responsible for losses which may occur in the purchase, sale or transaction of items due to the information contained herein. The possibility of errors associated with a work of this size always exists. The Authors respectfully request readers to inform them of any errors which may be disclosed, in order to make the appropriate corrections for future editions.

The Complete Price Guide to Antique Jewelry is published independently and is not associated with any jewelry manufacturer.

Ashland Publications
Suite 200
640 South Washington Blvd.
Sarasota Florida 34236

Library of Congress number 98-073605
ISBN 0-9666867-0-5

ACKNOWLEDGMENTS

The authors are especially appreciative of Chris Belliveau for his graphic art, layout and design work. A special thanks is also extended to Tom Dodson for the many expert photographs used in this book. The authors also thank Laurel McCullon-Wolf for her support and many hours of assistance as well as Deonnah Belliveau for her encouragement and support.

Send comments, additional information and corrections to James H. Wolf, Ashland Investments, 640 S. Washington Blvd. Suite 200,Sarasota, Florida 34236.

TABLE OF CONTENTS

ABOUT THE AUTHORS

The Complete Price Guide to Antique Jewelry is co-authored By Richard E. Gilbert and James H. Wolf.

Richard Gilbert is the owner of Ashland Investments, an international mail order business founded in 1963 which specializes in antique jewelry, pocket watches and vintage wrist watches. Mr. Gilbert holds both Bachelor and Masters degrees in Science. He has been a leading dealer and authority on watches and jewelry for over 35 years. His expertise and opinions are sought after by other dealers and major collectors. Mr. Gilbert is a co-author of the "Complete Price Guide to Watches", along with Mr. Cooksey Shugart. This book has been published and updated on an annual basis since 1979 and is recognized as the professional standard of watch price guides.

Mr. Wolf holds a Bachelors degree in fine arts and has been involved in the antique watch and jewelry market since 1979 as Manager of Sales for Ashland Investments. He serves as a special consultant on values and information listed in the "Complete Price Guide to Watches". Mr. Wolf has also produced over 50 specialty catalogs which are designed to market antique jewelry, vintage wristwatches and pocket watches to collectors throughout the world. This catalog series has become the most respected of its kind in the business.

The authors are long-standing members of the NAWCC (National Association of Watch & Clock Collectors) and they are considered foremost experts in the field of horology and vertu. The authors travel extensively to major auctions throughout the Untied States and Europe. They also attend regional and national conventions and shows.

Through the years, they have continued to expand their reference library which contains complete jewelry and watch auction results for the past 25 years as well as many rare books and articles on jewelry, horology and vertu. The authors keep an up-to-date pulse on the jewelry and watch market through the daily business transactions of Ashland Investments.

It is the authors' hope that this book will become the most widely used and authoritative book devoted to the antique jewelry market. Each additional edition will be thoroughly updated and expanded to keep pace with the market.

Any collector or dealer interested in antique jewelry, watches or objects of vertu are cordially invited to contact Ashland Investments and the offices of Mr. Gilbert and Mr. Wolf. Appointments are necessary. Ashland Investments is located in Sarasota Florida at 640 S. Washington Boulevard Suite 200, Sarasota, Florida 34236, telephone (941) 957-3760 or (800) 424-5353, fax (941) 365-4931.

INTRODUCTION

This book was created because the authors recognized that there was a tremendous need for a definitive edition which lists genuine values for antique jewelry. Since styles, types and varieties of jewelry are many, the book will include numerous photographs to show a broad range of items at all price levels. The text is designed to present basic information which is geared towards the antique jewelry collector's field and not the modern jewelry market. The Complete Price Guide to Antique Jewelry does not attempt to fix prices in the jewelry industry or trade market; rather, it reflects the buying and selling trends in the collectors market during the past year.

Hopefully, the book will give collectors both the confidence and knowledge they need to assist in their purchases. The information will also help to determine the value of family heirlooms. Dealers will find the book indispensable when researching buy and sell levels for estate jewelry. The publication will list major jewelry categories; cross references will be indicated when items may fall into more than one category. Comparative values should be used if an exact item is not found in the book.

Condition, age, quality of design and materials are important factors to be considered when making any decisions on the value of jewelry. The prices listed in this book are based on sales information and data which has been collected and analyzed from many dealers price lists and auction houses throughout the world. The prices should serve as a guide to the collector. The price you pay for jewelry will be determined by several factors including condition, rarity, stylistic character and design.
The authors plan to expand and improve this book on an annual basis. Prices will be re-evaluated to keep pace with current market levels. Additionally, other jewelry pieces which surface will also be featured. Informational text will be augmented and the text will be expanded.

It is the authors' hope that this edition will make your collecting ventures more pleasurable and profitable.

COLLECTING ANTIQUE JEWELRY

Antique jewelry has proven to be a highly collectible commodity which will hold its value and increase over time. The international appeal of jewelry makes it a viable investment as well as an enjoyable field of collecting. The craftsmanship and uniqueness of design exhibited in fine antique pieces cannot be matched by today's mass-produced medium and low-end jewelry examples.

Vintage jewelry, which was principally made from 1875 to 1950 is being purchased by people as usable pieces to wear and to keep as collectible treasures. The potential monetary appreciation and value which antique jewelry holds is directly related to the limited number of pieces which have survived through the years. High-end and moderately priced jewelry is constantly being purchased by dealers and then sold to collectors. As the years pass, this process makes period and collectible jewelry more difficult to find in the hands of the non-collecting public. When the supply dwindles, the prices for antique jewelry steadily rise. Due to the fine craftsmanship and uniqueness of design, antique jewelry also holds a high intrinsic value. This keeps it well above the bullion or "break down" value of the raw materials.

Antique jewelry can be collected and purchased in all price ranges. This makes the field easy to enter and allows collectors to be able to upgrade their investments as their income and knowledge increase. It is best to focus on period pieces which appeal to you. Also look for unique designs and pieces which are in top condition.

Reputable dealers can be found throughout the world. Shows, auctions and estate sales are also frequently held and they feature many fine pieces of antique and estate jewelry. As with any collectible field, the buyer must know and trust the reputation of the seller and all jewelry pieces should be properly represented. The best indication of value you can get as a collector will be provided by determining the original cost in materials and time it took to create an antique piece when it was originally made. As with today's jewelry, the jewelry of the past was produced in various levels of quality. Always look for the best stones, the finest mounts, exceptional designs and pieces which generally exhibit fine attention to detail.

JEWELRY PERIODS AND STYLES

The majority of antique jewelry available in today's market will fall into the following periods:

GEORGIAN PERIOD: 1790–1840's, Examples from this early period are highly collectible. The Georgian style flourished in the 1830's. Rose–cut diamonds, seed pearls, black and white enameled accents and spectacular high relief lava cameos are typical of the style and designs which were most popular. Mounts and frames were often high karat gold and ornamented with Greek key designs, acorn and leaf patterns and other neo–classical motifs. Georgian items are difficult to find unless established collections are liquidated.

GEORGIAN CAMEO

VICTORIAN EARRINGS

VICTORIAN: Victorian jewelry was produced during the reign of Britain's Queen Victoria, from 1837–1901. This period reached its peak in the latter part of the century. The styles of the Victorian era favored floral adornments, fine filigree work, blue and black enamel accents and mesh chain with a "woven" pattern. Dark–colored stones such as onyx and bloodstone were popular and platinum became the predominant metal of choice for mounts and better pins. Gypsy mounts were used for faceted stones and cabochons became more widely used. Stickpins, filigree bar pins, sport motif jewelry, crescent shapes and insect pins were all popular in the late Victorian era.

EDWARDIAN NECKLACE

EDWARDIAN: Edwardian jewelry refers to jewelry which was popular during the reign of King Edward III, from 1901–1910. This period is often an overlap of the Victorian era. Millegrain settings and a combination of platinum over gold were often used for settings and pins. Draped garland ornaments and guilloche enamels were popular. European cut diamonds, tourmalines, amethyst and garnets were primary stones of the period.

ART NOUVEAU BROOCH

ART NOUVEAU: Art Nouveau jewelry exhibits the fabulous free–flowing style which was in vogue from 1895–1915. Examples from this period are highly collectible. The term Art Nouveau means "new art". It represented figural images, flowers and insects. Enameling was very popular for adding brilliant colors to jewelry in this period. The delicate examples with plique–a–jour enamel from this time are highly prized by collectors and investors. Yellow gold came back in vogue and the trend was generally a lighter and more flowing sense of design, rather than the heavier styles used in the Victorian era. The "softer" stones were used more during this period with pearls, opals, amber and coral being among the most popular.

6

ART DECO PENDANT

ART DECO: Examples from the Art Deco period are some of the strongest and most desired pieces in the market. The period is characterized by geometric styles and designs. The Art Deco era dates from 1910–1930. The mid–1920's were the peak time for Deco popularity. Colors became more prominent in the Deco period–rubies, emeralds and sapphires were brought to the forefront and strong color contrast was combined with geometric shapes and abstract designs. Pave and channel set mounts gained in popularity with white gold and platinum being the metal color of choice. Colorful beads, line bracelets and fabulous diamond clip brooches were in vogue. Another highly collectible design period surfaced at the this time–the Egyptian Revival Period. The Egyptian Period traces its roots from 1922 when Howard Carter, a famous archeologist, discovered the tomb of King Tutankhamen. The Egyptian jewelry pieces used scarabs, pyramid designs, hieroglyphic patterns and other motifs. Turquoise,enamel, coral and lapis lazuli were commonly used in the Egyptian Period.

RETRO PERIOD: 1940–1950's, Jewelry from this period was produced in large, three dimensional styling which often used rose and green
gold mounts and links. Ruby and diamond combinations were in fashion
and baguette cuts were popular, along with star rubies, star sapphires and
other cabochons. Jewelry of this period was also influenced by World War
II: pearls were difficult to get from the Japanese markets and they tem-
porarily fell out of fashion. The Cartier "tank" styling became popular as
exhibited in the design of gents and ladies rectangular wristwatches.

RETRO RING

POST RETRO PERIOD: Late 1950's–1960's. Yellow gold, pearls,
cluster rings, charm bracelets and big, bold pins were the signs of the time.
Jewelry trends were toward pieces which could be worn "every day" and
not just for special occasions. Chains, bracelets, "Tiffany" solitaire rings
and gent's rings and accessories were all being marketed on a larger scale
than ever before.

POST RETRO RING

Jewelry which is signed by a recognized maker will always be more desireable than an unsigned piece. The piece will be bring a premium because of the signature especially when it is the work of an important designer or a piece which was handled by one of the more important houses. This section of the book is a "work in progress" and the authors welcome any additional information which readers may wish to share. The specific marks and signature styles used by jewelers will be expanded in the future editions of this book.

Adler
Geneva firm founded in 1886 byJacques Adler, works were influenced by eastern (Istanbul, Turkey) designs and motifs.
signature style--- Adler
numbered----no

Asprey & Co
London firm founded in 1781 by William Asprey specialties were gold boxes, silver and fine gold jewelry.
signature style---- Asprey
numbered----no

Bailey, Banks & Biddle
founded in 1878,Philadelphia firm with numerous branches.
signature style--- B B B
numbered--- yes

Black, Starr & Frost
long standing jewelry house dating back to the early 1800's. New York based.
signature style---B. S. & F.
numbered--- usually no

Boivin, Rene
Paris 1864-1917, prolific designer circa 1900, known for animal and nature motifs.
signature style---Rene Boivin, usually with French assay marks
numbered----no

Boucheron
founded 1858 by Frederic Boucheron, fine Paris jewelry house,
signature style--- Boucheron, Boucheron Paris
numbered--- sometimes

Buccellati

international firm founded in Milan 1919 by Mario Buccellati.
signature styles--Buccellati, M.Buccellati, Gianmaria Buccellati
numbered--- sometimes

Bulgari

founded in Rome 1879 by Sotirio Bulgari, known for classical and Renaissance influences
signature style--- Bulgari, Bulgari Roma
numbered---no

Caldwell, J. E. & Co

jewelry firm established in the mid 1800's, originally ,in Philadelphia, offered fine jewelry, watches and silver.
signature style---J E C & Co, also Caldwell
numbered---generally yes

Cartier

the "premier" name in jewelry, founded in 1847, Paris, by Louis Francois Cartier. The firm contin ued under Alfred Cartier and his three sons- Louis, Pierre, and Jacques. World wide acclaim was given to works and designs by Louis Cartier including magnificent Mystery clocks, wrist watchs, Art Deco jewelry and jewelry with Oriental designs.
signature styles--Cartier, Cartier Paris, Cartier London, Cartier New York
numbered--- yes

Charlton & Co.

New York jewelry house active from 1909 to the 1930's.
signature style---Charlton & Co
numbered---no

Chaumet

Paris firm headed by Joseph Chaumet producing award winning pieces from 1885 to 1934
signature style--- Chaumet Paris, France. Pieces also stamped with makers mark
numbered--- generally no

Cohen, Julius

Prominent jeweler, work with Oscar Heyman & Co in 1929 and Harry Winston in the 1940's.
signature style---Julius Cohen
numbered--- no

Dreicer & Co

early 1900's, New York and Chicago, rekown jeweler specializing in diamond and platinum jewels, influenced by Cartier and other Parisian styles.
signature style--- Dreicer & Co
numbered--- no

Falize

Important Paris workshop established by Alexis Falize (1811-1898) later run by his son Lucien and then his son Andre (1872-1936) Known for fine Art Nouveau and enamel pieces.
signature style--- no info
numbered--- no info

Flato, Paul

foremost American designer and jeweler, born 1900, shops in New York and Beverly Hills, Flato's jewels were favored by the Hollywood stars of the 1930's and 40's.
signature style--- Flato
numbered--- no

Fouquet, Georges

Parisian jeweler (1862-1957) associated with the artist and designer Alphonse Mucha, favored Art Nouveau style and enamel jewelry
signature style-- jeweller's mark
numbered--- yes

Gaillard, Lucien

Paris maker of fine enamels, influenced by Lalique and Japanese metal work styles produced award winning jewels from 1900- 1930
signature style--- L. Gallaird
numbered--- no

Gattle & Co E. M.

fine jewelers and goldsmiths, produced from 1900 to 1940, New York
signature style---Gattle
numbered--- no

Giuliano

Carlo (1831-1895) and his sons Arthur and Carlo were reknown London based jewelers specializing in Renaissance style creations.
signature style--- C. G. (early style for Carlo Giuliano) also: C & A G in an impressed oval (later mark for Carlo and Arthur Giuliano)
numbered--- no

11

Gubelin

founded in 1854, Swiss firm specializing in supe
rior quality watches, clocks and jewels.
signature style--- French assay marks and jew
elers marks for Gubelin
numbered--- sometimes

Oscar Heyman & Bros.

founded in 1912, New York jewelry firm
reknown for creations using fine precious stones
signature style--- OHB
numbered--- sometimes

Janesich, Leopoldo

famous maker of fine jewels and vanity cases for
the Royalty. First in Trieste, Italy and then Paris
signature style--- Janesich
numbered--- yes

Jay

designer J. Jay, born 1916, used diamonds and
precious colored stones, London and Far East
locations
signature style--- Jay
numbered---generally not

Lacloche Freres

founded in 1897, fine jewelry firm in Paris,
known for many fine Art Deco pieces in the
1920's.
signature styles--- Lacloche Freres , J.Lacloche,
Paris
numbered--- sometimes

Lalique, Rene

Lalique (1860-1945) was the premier maker of
rare Art Nouveau jewelry at the turn of the centu
ry. His work was both innovative and important.
Popular themes included nature, animal and
female figure motifs. Lalique also worked with
unusual materials such as rock crystal, horn,
glass and enamels.
signature style---jewelers mark
numbered--generally no

Lambert Brothers

A New York firm founded in 1877, they sold plat
inum and gold jewelry, watches, clocks and silver
items.
signature style--- Lambert
numbered--- no

Laykin & Cie	founded in 1935 by S. W. Laykin in Los Angeles, jewelry firm, associated with I. Magin branches. signature style--- Laykin numbered--- generally no
Marcus & Co	a twentieth century New York house which pro duced interesting enameled jewelry items during the Art Nouveau period. signature styles---M & Co, also Marcus & Co numbered--- sometimes
Mauboussin	Paris jewelry house founded by George Mauboussin in 1896. a major exhibitor of jewels during the 1920's. Later this firm merged with Trabert & Hoffer. signature style---French assay marks, makers mark numbered-- yes
Mellerio	Paris based, with a long history of fine jewelry, prominent exhibitors at Paris in 1867, 1878 and 1900 as well as the 1939 World's Fair in New York. signature style--- Mellerio, R. Paix, Paris numbered--- yes
Peacock C. D.	long standing jewelry firm tracing it's roots back to 1837 when Elijah Peacock opened a small shop in Chicago. signature styles-- Peacock or C. D. Peacock numbered--- no
Schlumberger, Jean	1907-1987, foremost designer for Tiffany & Co. Schlumberger was one of the first to be allowed to add his name to pieces made by Tiffany. signature style--- Tiffany, Schlumberger numbered--- sometimes

Seaman Schepps   born 1881, a unique designer and jeweler, early shops were located in California, later in New York. combined precious and semi-precious gems in highly colorful jewelry designs, also used natural shells, coral branches and ivory materials with gemstones.
signature styles--- Seaman Schepps, also P. S. V. of Seaman Schepps
numbered--- generally no

Shreve, Crump & Low Boston based retailer of fine jewelry with roots tracing back to 1796.
signature style--- S. C. & L. Co.
numbered--- no

Starr, Theodore B.   founded a jewelry store in 1862, New York. Exhibited pieces at the 1876 Philadelphia Centennial. The shop was closed in 1923.
signature style--- T. B. Starr Inc.
numbered--- no

Tiffany & Co   recognized as one of the finest names in the jewelry business, this New York house was founded in 1837 by Charles L. Tiffany and John B. Young. The firm was headed by Tiffany's son Louis Comfort Tiffany from 1902 to 1933. The Tiffany firm achieved international acclaim with the use of innovative designs, fine craftsmanship and quality gems.
signature styles--- Tiffany, Tiffany & Co, T & Co
Note: from 1870 to the 1890's many early pieces were signed "Tiffany" on one line and "& Co" below (on the next line).
numbered--- sometimes

Trabert & Hoeffer   New York firm founded in the 1930's, they formed a partnership with the Parisian firm Mauboussin.
signature styles-- Trabert & Hoeffer, Mauboussin T & H M "Reflection" (this signature is found on a unique line of jewelry produced in the 1930's)
numbered--- sometimes

Van Cleef & Arpels	founded in 1906, prestigious French firm which expanded to become one of the leading jewelry firms worldwide. Introduced the "invisible mount ing" for gems in the mid 1930's. signature styles---VCA, V.C.A. Van Cleef & Arpels numbered--- sometimes
Webb, David	1912-1975, New York based, Webb was the most highly acclaimed American designer. His works were influenced by ancient Greek and Roman forms as well as classical jewelry styles. His designs often featured exotic non-traditional colored stones. Webb was also reknown for exquisite enamel and precious stone animal-form jewelry. signature styles-- Webb, David Webb numbered--- no
Winston, Harry	1896-1978, New York, Harry Winston is often referred to as the most important diamond and precious gem dealer and connoisseur in the world. Winston handled the most important dia monds and gems. He was famous for recutting old European cut stones and then creating excit ing new jewelry designs. signature style---Winston numbered---sometimes
Yard, Raymond C.	1885-1958, important jeweler, his New York firm established a reputation for having only the finest quality pieces, all of which were hand crafted for their prominent clientele. signature style--- Yard numbered--- no

ANTIQUE JEWELRY
Outstanding values
on fine estate jewelry.

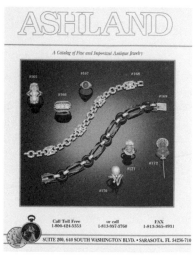

The Ashland color catalog series includes some of the finest antique jewelry ever made, at the best prices.It is a must for the avid collector and fine jewelry lover.

ASHLAND ALSO OFFERS AN EVERY OTHER MONTH BLACK AND WHITE LIST WITH A COLOR INSERT. CONTAINING 200 PIECES OF ESTATE AND ANTIQUE JEWELRY, WITH AN EXCITING AUCTION STYLE BID SHEET FOR ITEMS THAT DO NOT SELL AT LIST PRICE

If you would like to recieve these catalogs free of charge call or write to:

ASHLAND
INVESTMENTS

640 S. WASHINGTON BLVD.
SUITE 200
SARASOTA FL. 34236
(941) 957-3760 1-800-424-5353

16

MARKET REPORT

The demand for good antique jewelry became even stronger in 1999 and dealers had no trouble placing better pieces.

The inflation rate was relatively low and the gold and silver market was still soft at mid–year with gold trading in the $295 range per ounce. Fortunately, the antique jewelry market is not heavily influenced by the price level of gold. The jewelry market was very lively as collectors pursued better quality and interesting pieces. Early Victorian pieces remained strong and the most frequently asked for items were longer drop earrings, Art Nouveau lavalieres and bracelets with age, character and flair.

The requests for larger diamonds remained strong. Quality emeralds, sapphires and rubies were also widely sought after. Period pieces, larger pearl chokers, and jade were all very much desired. Cameos prices were up with a marked increase in demand for better hardstone examples and early high quality pieces. Important enamelled jewelry is becoming very scarce. Premier examples of fine enamelling are very strong.

The only slow areas of the market were smaller pearl goods, diamond clusters, stickpins and some retro period pieces.

The upsurge of online Internet auctions has added a new dimension to the world of collecting. This mass expansion of the marketplace will lead to higher prices as the finer antique jewelry items become more widely dispersed throughout the world. The authors will monitor this new and exciting medium closely, and expand on the impact of the Internet in the next edition.

PRECIOUS METALS USED IN JEWELRY

Collectible jewelry is most often found in gold or platinum settings. These precious metals are used in jewelry–making due to their workability, luster, color and virtual indestructibility.

Gold is too soft in its pure form, so it is alloyed with other metals, principally silver and copper. Rose, white, green, yellow and other colorful shades of gold can be produced by combining various mixtures of alloy metals with the pure gold.

Although similar in appearance to silver, platinum has a look and luster which is unique. Platinum does not tarnish and it's strength and malleability are prime factors in its popular use in filigree work. Platinum filigree work is highly desirable and always in demand. The use of platinum for mounting diamonds became popular in the early 1900's; the metal's luster and color would enhance the diamond's reflective properties.

GOLD FINENESS OR KARAT: Gold in its purest form is 24 karat. It is normally weighed in troy ounces with 20 pennyweights (dwts) equaling one ounce. The most widely used fineness mixtures of gold used in jewelry are 9K, 10K, 14K and 18K. The karat of gold is determined by the amount of metal alloy which is added to the pure gold.

FINENESS CHART
(Percentage of 1,000 parts)

9K	.3750
10K	.4167
12K	.5000
14K	.5833
15K	.6250
18K	.7500
20K	.8333
22K	.9167
24K	1.000

Multi–colored gold is created by varying the alloy metals used with pure gold. Silver is the alloy which is generally used for white gold and copper is used for red and rose gold. Blue, green and violet shades of gold are also found. These are produced by adding elements such as iron, nickel, zinc and palladium to the gold.

Contemporary gold is often measured in grams. To convert grams to pennyweights, multiply grams times .6431 to equal dwts (pennyweights). The following chart shows standard gold measures and weights.

1 Troy Ounce =	20 Pennyweight (Dwt)
1 Troy Ounce =	31.1033 Grams
12 Troy Ounces =	1 Pound Troy
14.5833 Troy Ounces =	1 Pound Avoirdupois
0.9114 Troy Ounce =	1 Ounce Avoirdupois
32.15 Troy Ounces =	1 Kilogram
1 Gram =	0.643 Pennyweight (dwt)
1.5552 Grams =	1 Pennyweight (dwt)
1000 Grams =	1 Kilogram
240 Pennyweight (dwt) =	1 Pound Troy
643.01 Pennyweight (dwt) =	1 Kilogram
18.2291 Pennyweight (dwt) =	1 Ounce Avoirdupois

Bullion values or the "scrap" value of gold is important in determining the base melt value which heavy gold objects such as bracelets, boxes and chains have in gold weight. The following formulas are easy to use multiples which will give the bullion value that a refiner will pay for one dwt of gold in various karats. "Spot" is the daily quote given for one troy ounce of pure gold. The "spot" price fluctuates daily.

Let's assume that gold spot is $300 per ounce. To determine the melt price of one dwt of 18K gold, the following formula would be used:

$300 (Spot) x .750 (18K fineness) = $225
$225 divided by 20 dwts per ounce = $11.25
$11.25 less 6% (the refiner's cost and commission) = $10.57 which gives you the price one dwt of 18K will bring.

Platinum is valued by the ounce or pennyweight and it brings a premium if found as a useable mount or filigree frame or pin. Platinum is usually alloyed with iridium and jewelry pieces are commonly marked 10%irid/plat.

Silver, brass and copper are metals also used in antique jewelry making. Gold–filled and gilt metal (gold on silver) or gold on brass were also used for antique frames and mounts.

Jewelry found in these metals are generally not as desirable as those produced in gold or platinum. Very early pieces, scarce items and some signed pieces (such as Georg Jensen, a noted designer specializing in sterling pieces) are the exceptions to this rule.

COMMONLY SEEN METAL MARKS
PRECIOUS METALS

.750	18K gold
.585	14K gold
.375	9K gold
Irid	Iridium
Pall	Palladium
Plat	Platinum
.925	Sterling silver

NON–PRECIOUS METALS

1/10 12K	Gold filled
10K or 14K HGE	Heavy gold electroplate
RGP	Rolled gold plate
Warranted 10 years/25 years	Gold–filled
EPNS	Electroplated Nickel Silver

DIAMONDS

The diamond has and always will be the "premier" gemstone used in jewelry. The study of diamonds will fill complete volumes and many years of research and experience are needed to become a true expert. However, the jewelry lover and collector can easily learn the basics of diamond values and grading by reading the many fine articles and books on the subject and above all, by viewing and comparing as many diamonds as possible.

The four "C's" are the primary aspects to consider when viewing and grading a diamond. They are:

> Carat weight
> Cut
> Clarity
> Color

The carat (ct) is a unit of weight and not a unit of size. This standard unit of weight is used for all gemstones: one carat weighs 200 milligrams, or 1/5 of a gram.

The carat weight of diamonds are also referred to by a number of points, a one carat diamond weighs 100 points. Therefore, a half carat diamond (.50 ct) would be referred to as fifty points and a smaller diamond of one–fifth of a carat would be .20 ct or a twenty point stone.

Diamond melee is a term used to describe small diamonds which range from .01 ct (one point) to .25 ct (twenty five points).

CARAT

The true carat weight of a stone can only be determined when the stone is unmounted and placed on a gem lab–quality scale. Most stones that the collector will encounter in settings have to be approximated as to weight. This is generally done by using a spread gauge which relates the diameter of a stone to an approximate carat weight.This "estimated" weight is possible because diamonds are proportionately cut with the same percentages making up the table, crown, and pavillion surfaces.

A more accurate estimate of weight can be obtained by the use of a specialty gauge such as a Leveridge gauge, which can measure diameter, depth and width. A gauge of this type is indispensable in estimating pear, marquis and other fancy–shaped stones.

The formulas and charts used to determine weight are helpful—but the collector must keep in mind that they are only close approximations. A chart showing the sizes and weights of round diamonds will appear at the end of this section.

CUT

The cut of a diamond is one of the most important factors which determines the amount of fire or brilliance the stone will show.

Cut does not refer to the overall shape of a stone (examples: round, pear, marquise). The term refers to the proportions, symmetry, finish and polish the stone has. Diamonds which are not cut to good proportion or those with chips on the table, girdle or culet will be substantially devalued. Shallow, heavy and out of round cuts are also not desirable. A well–cut diamond will give maximum brilliance as light is internally reflected from facet to facet and then reflected out through the top of the stone. When a diamond is cut too deep or too shallow, the light will be reflected to some extent, out the bottom of the stone. Brilliance will be lost and the center of the diamond will appear dark, watery or glassy.

The terms used to show the major cuts or facets on a diamond are:

Table: the "table" is the large facet which tops the gemstone

Crown: the facets which are between the table and the center or "girdle" of the stone

Girdle: the center "line" of a diamond between the upper crown and the lower pavilion

Pavilion: the facets or cuts below the center or girdle

Culet: the bottom "point" or lowermost part of the faceted stone

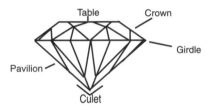

There are numerous diamond cuts and variations which have been used through the years. The most commonly seen cuts which the antique jewelry collector will encounter will be listed here.

Table or rough cut:
The simplest and earliest form of cutting where a top point of the stone would be polished flat to create a larger square surface or table.

Rose cut:
An early cut in which the diamond has a flat base with facets starting from a top point which spread towards the edge of the stone, usually in multiples of six.

Cushion cut:
Also referred to as Mine Cut; this style has a cushion or squarish shape when the outer edge is viewed from the top. The stone is cut with a smaller top table, a high crown and a very deep pavilion. The culet does not come to a point, rather it is flat on the bottom. This flat and large culet can be viewed through the top of the stone as what many people call a "fish–eye" effect.

European cut:

Along with the cushion cut, the European cut was the forerunner of the brilliant cut diamonds of today. The European cut stone appeared in the 1850's and it was widely used until the 1930's. The European cut is round and much more evenly proportioned than the old mine cuts. The culet is flat but less pronounced than the broader culet of the old cushion cut.

American Brilliant cut:

The American or "modern" brilliant cut round diamond has 58 facets and a closed or "pointed" culet. The ideal cut has 32 facets above the table and 24 facets below.

Single cut:

These diamonds are generally small melee (.01 to .25 ct) which are cut with 16 facets and used as "ornamental" side stones or in items such as ladies' watch bands.

CLARITY

The clarity of a diamond can greatly influence its value and collectibility. The standard GIA (Gemological Institute of America) clarity scale will be shown at the end of this section. When examining a diamond, a 10 power loupe (available at jewelry supply houses, hobby shops, etc.) should be used. While using a loupe, you should examine the stone in good light from the top and all side angles for imperfections or blemishes. The term"inclusions" refers to internal flaws in the diamond crystal. Common flaws are:

Bubbles: small hollow specks usually in the body of the stone, caused by air formation while crystallizing.

Carbon spots: black specks which can vary in size, large spots visible to the naked eye are much more detrimental than those barely visible.

Clouds: a cluster of white inclusions, generally small white crystals

Feathers: a milky flake formed in crystallization, also a white cleav - age or fracture line formed in the body of the stone. They can cause haziness and lack of brilliance, depending upon severity.

Fracture: a break or chip in the stone which appears in a direction other than a cleavage plane

Girdle chips: small chips can appear through heavy wear or careless mounting. The girdle can be "brittle" due to its fine edge. **NOTE:** Chips are often "hidden" by placing them under the prongs. Rough edges or overly thick edges will also cast a shadow through the stone, causing a loss of brilliance.

Scratches: minor table or crown scratches can be polished out. Major scratches are much more of a serious flaw.

"Eye clean" is a term often used to describe a diamond which has no visible flaws to the naked eye.

The clarity scale is broken down into the following grades:

F **Flawless**
Free from all inclusions or blemishes

IF **Internally Flawless**
No inclusions visible at 10x magnification

VVS1 **Very Very Slight Inclusion #1**
Inclusions that are extremely difficult to locate at 10x

VVS2 **Very Very Slight Inclusion #2**
Inclusions that are very difficult to locate at 10x

VS1 **Very Slight Inclusion #1**
Minor inclusions that are difficult to locate at 10x

VS2 **Very Slight Inclusion #2**
Minor inclusions that are somewhat difficult to locate at 10x

SI1 **Slight Inclusion #1**
Noticeable inclusions that are easy to locate at 10x

SI2 **Slight Inclusion #2**
Noticeable inclusions that are very easy to locate at 10x. Some inclusions may be seen with the unaided eye.

I1 **Inclusion #1**
Obvious inclusions– Somewhat easy to see with unaided eye.

Victorian bracelet and brooch, sapphire ring, diamond and ruby ring, Art Deco diamond ring, ruby and gold cufflinks

Victorian brooch with enamel, two antique cross pendants, sapphire and dia-
mond bar pin, early Victorian bracelet
NEXT PAGE
A rare Cartier lapis, turquoise and gold necklace
Diamond earrings, sapphire earrings, Art Deco pendant,
Retro aquamarine ring

A collection of rare enameled pins c. 1870-1910

I2   **Inclusion #2**
         Obvious inclusions– easy to locate with the unaided eye.

I3   **Inclusion #3**
         Obvious inclusions– very easy to see with the unaided eye.

COLOR

When seen from a distance, the first characteristic a diamond shows is its "color". Although the "colorless" or "white" diamonds are the finest, the majority will show some hint of yellow shading or a brownish or grey tint. In determining the "color" of a diamond, you should always view the stone through the side and not from the top. Many near colorless diamonds are said to "face up" very strong,this term refers to the absence of yellow shades the diamond reflects when viewed from the top. Yet, the same stone will show traces of color when viewed from the side.True fancy color diamonds are rare and valuable–they range from intense yellows (canary) to blue, brown, green, pinks and reds. The color a diamond has can be altered by irradiation treatments and heating techniques. Proper certifications, appraisals and laboratory gem testing results should always be presented with the sale of a "natural" rare fancy–colored diamond.The body color a diamond possesses is determined by the amount of yellow or brown tint which can be seen in the colorless stone. The standard GIA Color Grading Scale shown below is universally used in the jewelry markets.

GIA COLOR GRADING SCALE

D E F	G H I J	K L M N	O P Q R S	T U V	W X Y Z
colorless	near colorless	faint yellow	very light yellow	light yellow	fancy yellow

"Colorless" stones are very rare and diamonds in this ranking (D, E and F) command a premium. The G and H grade diamonds are referred to as "fine white" or near colorless. The very lightly tinted diamonds are represented in the I and J categories while K and L graded stones will show more easily viewed yellow or brown tints. The remaining grades, M–Z, will exhibit more tint as the grades progress. "Cape" diamonds are those showing a stronger color tint.The color and type of setting or mount can influence the color a diamond shows, therefore, truly accurate gradings can only be achieved when the stone is loose. Soap, grease and dirt will build up in diamond mounts and drastically reduce the brilliance or whiteness a stone will show when it is properly cleaned.

DIAMOND SHAPES

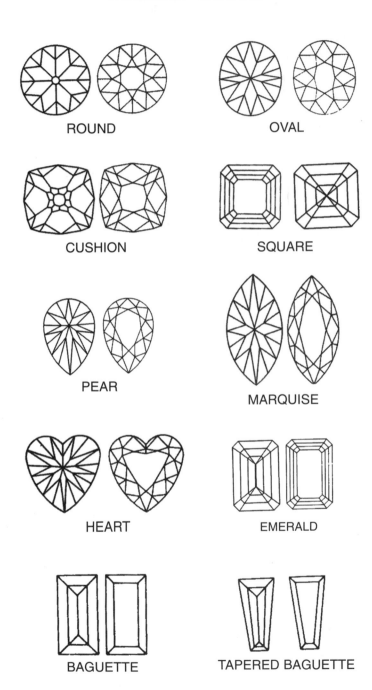

ROUND

OVAL

CUSHION

SQUARE

PEAR

MARQUISE

HEART

EMERALD

BAGUETTE

TAPERED BAGUETTE

ROUND DIAMOND SIZES

A true carat weight can only be determined when a diamond is unmounted and weighed. The following chart is only a guide to indicate the approximate diameter which a typical round diamond will show when viewed from the top.

Millimeter size (diameter)	Approx. carat weight
1.3	.01
1.7	.02
2.0	.03
2.2	.04
2.4	.05
2.7	.07
3.0	.10
3.4	.15
3.8	.20
4.1	.25
4.4	.33
4.7	.40
5.1	.50
5.8	.75
6.3	1.00

ROUND MILLIMETER SIZES

| 1 | 2 | 3 | 4 | 5 | 6 | 7 | 8 | 10 | 11 | 12 |

EMERALD, SAPPHIRE AND RUBY

When it comes to colored gemstones, these three jewels have always been the most popular, intriguing and valuable. Color has a natural and immediate appeal to the eye of every person and this attraction to color is really the main underlying basis on which the value is determined.

As with diamonds, the clarity, carat and cut are also strong factors in determining the value, yet color must be given priority when the stone is being judged.

Emeralds are a variety of the mineral beryl. Sapphires and rubies are both in the corundum family.

Color quality in these precious stones can vary greatly–the overall tone, depth of color, intensity, evenness of color and presence of secondary shades are all things to consider when the gems are being evaluated. The color which is shown can vary depending upon the light source (natural, fluorescent or incandescent).

When you view an "emerald green" gemstone or a "blue sapphire" or a "red ruby", there are almost always secondary shades or colors which come into play. Emeralds will show tints of yellow or blue. Rubies can range from very light pink shades to the famous "pigeon blood" red of prized Burmese rubies. Rubies will also exhibit tinges of purple, blue, orange or brown as an underlying color.

Sapphires can run the spectrum from very dark to light blue and they may have green undertones as a secondary hue.

NOTE: Attractive deep green sapphires are found in antique jewelry and if the shade is pleasing to the eye, they are quite desirable.

Again, we stress that the best way to become comfortable with colored stones is to view as many as possible with the "color" being your primary concern in determining which stone is more appealing. Also remember that very dark stones will hide flaws such as inclusions and feathers andgenerally, these are less valuable than lively transparent stones which are only slightly included or flawed.

Emeralds, rubies and sapphires are found in faceted cuts and in cabochons. In particular, the "star" rubies and sapphires are quite popular. Star sapphires and star rubies are prized for the hypnotic play of light or "austerism" which reflects from the stone. The star effect is produced by thin crystalline fibers or "rods" which are present in the stone. When the gem is cut "en cabochon", the reflection of light from these fibers can be seen on the surface. The resulting star effect is produced by the crossing of these internal reflective bands.

The "star's" color, symmetry, clarity and definition are all characteristics which are used to determine value. However, be aware that many synthetics are on the market. Due to the fact that doublets, synthetics and other "non–genuine" stones are often encountered, it is imperative that any "high priced" or rare colored gemstone be accompanied by legitimate laboratory reports and appraisals.

You will often see small baguette or triangle cut green, red and blue stones as side "accent" pieces in antique jewelry. In earlier times the jewelry makers found that genuine rubies, emeralds or sapphires were quite expensive and they often were not vibrant or strong in color. Therefore, nicely colored synthetics were used. This practice does not greatly reduce the value of an antique piece if the main stone is genuine.

A BRIEF SYNOPSIS OF COLORED GEMS

ALEXANDRITE: A rare gemstone, a variety of chrysoberyl. This transparent gem appears light to dark green in natural light and purplish–pink to red under artificial light. The stone is named after Alexander II of Russia. The most popular cut is a faceted step cut. Alexandrite is rare and valuable in larger sizes. Note: Beware of synthetics!

AMBER: This material is a natural resin or fossilized tree sap found in pale yellow, brown or reddish colors. A popular material for beads and earrings, amber is often imitated by plastics or green copal. Natural amber will burn with a white smoke and a pine scent. It becomes electromagnetic when rubbed. Small pieces of amber are pressed to form larger masses such as those used for amber pipe stems or cigarette holders.

AMETHYST: A crystalized quartz variety. Color ranges from pale violet to a very deep purple. Generally transparent and faceted or step cut. Amethyst is a moderately priced stone which was popular in all periods. Larger sizes with deep, pleasing color are especially desirable. The name is derived from the Greek "Amethustos" (not drunk) , the belief was that the wearing of the stone prevented intoxication.

AQUAMARINE: A variety of beryl, this stone is prized in large sizes which have deep blue coloring. The stone is often found with good clarity and colors can range from light/pale blue to green/blue to deeper blue. Synthetic colored spinels and blue topaz are less valuable color "substitutes" for genuine aquamarine. The name is derived from the Latin words for water and sea.

BLOODSTONE: A widely used stone for men's antique rings and fobs and it is often carved or cut as an intaglio. Bloodstone is a dark green quartz with specks of red found throughout. Bloodstone has been held as a "medicinal cure" stone throughout time.

CARNELIAN: This opaque stone is a chalcedony (variety of quartz) which was popular for producing antique seals, intaglios, cameos, fobs and boxes. Varies from reddish–orange to deep red. Carnelian is moderately hard and it takes a high polish.

CAT'S EYE: A variety of chrysoberyl. Normally cabochon cut, this gem produces an eye effect from a light or white line which runs down the center line of the stone. Colors include yellow, honey and green tones. A similar but lesser value stone is the Tiger's Eye, which is a variety of quartz.

CITRINE: Like amethyst, citrine is a member of the quartz family. The colors of citrine range from pale yellow to richer tones with brown shadings. The stone is moderate in value and it is not unusual to find citrine in larger sizes. The name is derived from the French "citron" which means lemon, a reference to citrine's color.

CORAL: A natural limestone formation which is found in white, pink, orange and red hues. Angel skin coral is a popular white variety which exhibits very soft pink or peach overtones or highlights. Oxblood coral is the rarest–a very intense red variety. Coral is carved or cabochon cut. Popular in antique Victorian pieces.

GARNET: This crystal ranges from transparent to opaque and is found in nearly every color except blue. Faceted and rose cut stones were popular in antique pins, earrings, necklaces and bracelets. The deep red variety of garnet is the most commonly seen shade. Garnets are relatively inexpensive and were widely used. An exception, however, is the Demantoid garnet–this variety is found in yellowish–green to rich emerald green colors and it commands a premium value. The word garnet is from the Latin word for pomegranate "granatum".

JADE: This hard stone can be found in all shades and degrees of green. Black, white, grey, brown and yellow jade are all found. The Chinese have held jade in high esteem for centuries. The term "jade" is used to describe both jadeite and nephrite—these two minerals differ in hardness and weight. Jadeite is more desirable than nephrite and the most prized examples are rich "Imperial Jade" which is emerald or apple green in color. Burmese jade is considered to be the finest. Nephrite is commonly used to form necklace beads and decorative carvings. Nephrite is generally darker than fine jadeite.

LAPIS LAZULI: A deep blue stone with gold flecks, lapis lazuli is opaque and its use was very popular during the Egyptian Revival Period. In antique pieces, it is found in cufflinks and rings–generally is a flat cut, polished stone.

MALACHITE: A soft stone with "stripes" or line patterns of deep green and copper ore. Used for boxes, beads and pendants. It is easily carved and polished.

MOONSTONE: An opalescent stone (feldspar variety). Shades range from milky or "cloudy" white to better stones showing tinges of blue. Normally cut in cabochon for rings. This translucent stone was prized by many fine Art Nouveau jewelers for its iridescent properties.

OPALS: This popular gem is usually cut flat or as a cabochon. The intensity of colors can vary greatly. Values are related to the brilliance of the colors, the evenness of dispersion and the "play" or "liveliness" shown by the stone. Opals with a predominant amount of blues or greens are the most often seen variety. An opal with strong reds and genuine "black" opals are more desirable. The black opal is generally regarded as the most brilliant and it is often imitated by cheaper "doublets". A doublet (or triplet) is actually a layered creation where parts are joined together to form a larger stone. The thin layer of genuine stone is fused together with glass or other non–precious materials. The term "jelly opal" is used to describe clear or pale opals which are nearly transparent; these are generally not high in value. Opals are rather fragile stones, they can easily crack and they are heat–sensitive. Opals should not be immersed in hot water or cleaned in an ultrasonic.

PEARLS:Please refer to PEARL SECTION

PERIDOT : This transparent stone is a variety of the mineral olivine. It generally has a yellowish–green color and the stone is usually faceted in a round or emerald cut. A unique characteristic of peridot is its "double refraction" property which will make the back facets appear to have two edges when the stone is viewed through the top table.

TOPAZ: Topaz is a very clean and hard stone which is found in color ranges from clear to yellow, yellow–brown, pink and blue. It is one of the harder gemstones–an 8 on the Moh's scale. Genuine topaz is often imitated by stones which are in the lower value quartz family, such as citrine and other varieties of yellow quartz. Gemological tests can quickly determine if a topaz is real. Topaz is usually faceted and a cut topaz will take a very high polish. It should also be noted that most "blue" topaz (especially deep blue varieties) have been treated to enhance the color.

TOURMALINE: This gemstone is found in a rainbow of colors–sometimes even two or three stones will appear in a single stone. Green tourmalines and popular pink/red tourmalines (rubellite) are often found in estate jewelry.

TURQUOISE: Genuine natural turquoise can be found in many shades of blue and with green and brown secondary tones. This opaque stone is rather soft and usually cut in cabochon. Better examples are more translucent and they show an intense uniform shade of blue. "Persian" turquoise is considered the finest. Lower grades of the stone will be more "waxy" in finish, greener in color and marked with numerous brownish matrix veins or patches.

GENERALLY ACCEPTED LIST OF BIRTH STONES

January	Garnet
February	Amethyst
March	Aquamarine or Bloodstone
April	Diamond
May	Emerald
June	Pearl, Moonstone or Alexandrite
July	Ruby
August	Peridot or Sardonyx
September	Sapphire
October	Opal or Tourmaline
November	Topaz or Smoky Quartz
December	Turquoise or Lapis Lazuli

ABBREVIATIONS USED IN THIS BOOK

c	Circa
cab	Cabochon
ct	Carat Weight (weight of diamonds and gemstones)
dwt	Pennyweight
ex	Excellent Condition
gf	Gold Filled
hc	Hunters case
j	Jewels in watches
k	Karat (Example: 14K, the level of gold fineness)
mm	Millimeter
nm	Near mint condition
of	Open face watch
plat	Platinum
sm	Small
Ster	Sterling
tw	Total weight
wg	White Gold
yg	Yellow Gold

MILLIMETER / INCH CONVERSIONS

The size of beads, pearls,and large stones will be referred to in millimeters.

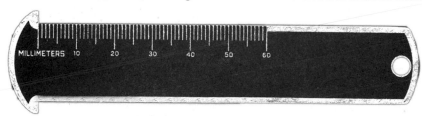

1 millimeter =	.0394 inches
1/4 inch =	6.35 millimeters
1/2 inch =	12.7 millimeters
3/4 inch =	19.05 millimeters
1 inch =	25.40 millimeters

GRADING LEVELS USED IN THIS BOOK

The majority of items photographed and described in this edition will be in near mint or better condition. Damaged jewelry is generally not desirable unless the damage is minute, easily repairable or the item is scarce and extremely collectible as a period piece. If a specific grade is not assigned to an item, then the reader may assume that the piece falls into the near mint category. Pieces which are assigned a premium value due to extraordinary condition will be graded mint or unused.

UNUSED: A piece which is virtually like new in all aspects.

MINT: An item showing very little use. Any small flaws should only be visible with the use of a loupe.

NEAR MINT: An extremely well–preserved piece, slight signs of use may be visible.

EXCELLENT: Presentable condition. Mounts and frames may need refurbishing. Stones may show some abrasions or scratches. Some previous repairs may be slightly notice able.

POOR: Readily visible damage to either stones and/or settings.

RARITY LEVELS AND THE STAR SYSTEM

Selected jewelry pieces will be assigned a star system which will indicate the relative scarcity of that particular piece. This grading system is designed to assist collectors and investors in determining the scarcity of a given piece in today's market.

A "one star" item is scarce and very collectible. The addition of more stars will increase in relation to the scarcity level with a "five star" ranking being the highest.

The star system will highlight items which offer a strong investment potential. The following factors are the basis of assigned rarity levels and star gradings:

A.   Market availability both past and present.

B.   Original quality of workmanship materials and innovative design.

C.   Historical importance.

D.   Condition in relation to other similar types which have surfaced in the marketplace.

E.   Artistic design, unusual shapes, forms and styles

F.   Low survival rate of similar types in good condition

G.   Investment potential for future increase in demand and value

H.   Signature pieces by reknown makers as well as unsigned pieces which strongly represent a period or style (i.e., Art Deco, Art Nouveau).

Stars will follow the prices.
Example:

Diamond and emerald brooch, 25x49 mm, forty-four diamonds (tw 8.25ct) 3.75 ct emerald at center, 12 dwts
c.1890   6000 10000 12000 ☆☆☆

PRICE LEVELS AND HOW TO USE THIS BOOK

This book has been structured to give the reader a "complete" sense of the various price levels which antique jewelry brings in today's market. All jewelry pieces are different and each item should be evaluated on an individual basis and in how it compares to the value of similar items. In the past, jewelry price guide books have shown numerous photos and each piece was assigned a value. This method would work well if you had an identical piece to that which was shown in the book, but this rarely happens since the subject matter is so wide in scope and each piece is somewhat different from any other. The primary goal of this book is to help the reader become more confident with the value of all estate and antique jewelry items. Therefore, in order to give the reader a better overall "feel" or sense of price levels, the authors have taken a different approach.

The individual sections will have a general price listing at the beginning. This master list will show all of the various jewelry styles for that section. The master list will be accompanied by general price tips and pricing information which is pertinent to that section. All prices will be listed in U. S. dollars. The photo examples will follow with similar items being presented together. The top of each page will show the main item and the style or type which is shown on that page (ie: Cameo brooch). Every individual photo example will be priced and described. The reader should compare the item they are evaluating to both the master price listings and the photo examples. This process will quickly give you a good "ball park" range of value. Small price adjustments should be allowed for since no two pieces are identical in terms of design or condition. It is also important to note that gold weights (pennyweights--dwts) will be listed with all gold jewelry entries where the gold value needs to be considered as a part of the overall value of the item. The gold weights used in the main sections will intentionally be kept to basic numbers which can easily be divided or multiplied--this will make it easy to relate gold values on a percentage basis with items of different weights. The photo examples will be listed with the actual weights of the items. The examples photographed in this book are all actual pieces which the authors have owned or handled at some time in the past few years. All information regarding these examples is accurate and up to date.

The jewelry prices shown will represent three levels. Listed from left to right these are:

1. Average Wholesale price---This level is the approximate dollar amount an item will bring when sold to a dealer or wholesale buyer. This level is for a piece which is saleable and not damaged.

2. Near Mint,Typical---This plateau is the market price which a piece should sell for in near mint or excellent condition. This level also represents the value of a jewelry item which is a" typical" example of the style described. The quality of the gemstones, the mountings, and the workmanship will be an average representation of the style.

3. Mint,Premium---The final level shows the top price a mint or premium quality piece will bring. This level is also an indication of a piece which shows superior quality in design, high grade gemstones or is a strong representative of a period. (Art Deco, Victorian etc.)

The prices listed in this book should be considered a general "guide" to value as the title suggests. As with any commodity, the market and retail prices will vary due to several factors such as advertising and inventory costs, regional differences in supply, currency exchange rates, and the ever changing supply and demand.

The authors of this work will always strive to keep the listed prices as current as possible and in line with the ever- changing market.

BRACELETS

Bracelets have always been one of the most popular jewelry forms. The styles can range from simple gold bangles to exotic gemstone link designs. In determining prices, the main consideration should be what the primary value relates to. In gold link, cuff and bangle designs the primary value will relate to the gold content. With gemstone and natural bead bracelets however, the value of the stones will be the primary aspect to consider. Once the primary value is established, you need look to design features (ie engraving, enameling, filigree work) which may enhance the look and therefore the price of a bracelet. The stones in diamond, sapphire, ruby and emerald bracelets can vary widely as far as color, quality, clarity and cut. The additional value which these stones add will be directly related to the quality of the gems. All bracelet examples listed in this section will be in gold or platinum and they will have gold clasps unless otherwise specified. The prices listed relate to the current gold market with gold spot being $295 per ounce at the time of this printing.

Diamond and pearl bracelet, 14k wg, forty-five diamonds
(tw 1.80 ct) 2.5 mm round pearls 18 dwts c.1920
1200 2000 2500 ☆☆

BRACELETS (NO GEMSTONES)

Bangle 3 mm wide plain 14k 5dwts	45	75	100
Bangle 3 mm wide plain 18k 5 dwts	55	100	125
Bangle 6 mm wide plain 14k 10 dwts	100	150	175
Bangle 6 mm wide plain 18k 10 dwts	125	200	225
Bangle 10 mm wide plain 14k 15 dwts	150	225	275
Bangle 10 mm wide plain 18k 15 dwts	200	300	350
Bangle 6 mm fancy engraved 14k 10 dwts	125	175	200
Bangle 6 mm enamel accents 14k 10 dwts	150	225	275
Bangle 6 mm 14k 10 dwts. 25 ct tw diamonds	175	250	300
Bangle 10 mm 18k15 dwt .50 ct tw diamonds	325	500	600
Cuff 15 mm plain 14k 10 dwts	100	175	225
Cuff 15 mm plain 18k 10 dwts	125	200	250
Cuff 20 mm plain 14k 15 dwts	150	250	300
Cuff 20 mm plain 18k 15 dwts	200	300	350
Cuff 15 mm fancy braided style 14k 30 dwts	350	450	500
Cuff very wide 1-1/2" 14k 40 dwts	400	600	700
Link standard 14k 10 dwts	85	150	200
Link standard 18k 10 dwts	125	175	225
Link standard 14k 20 dwts	175	300	400
Link standard 18k 20 dwts	250	350	450
LInk standard two tone 14k 10 dwts	100	175	225
Link standard two tone 18k 10 dwts	125	225	275
Link fancy engraved 14k 10 dwts	125	175	275
Link fancy engraved 18k 10 dwts	150	225	275
Link tube links 18k 20 dwts	250	400	500
Link open filigree 18k 20 dwts	300	400	500
Link heavy two tone 18k 40 dwts	650	800	900
Link multi strand 18k 70 dwts	800	1100	1300
Link flower form high relief 18k 20 dwts	400	600	700
Coin bracelet 22k coins 18k links 50 dwts	1000	1500	1800
Charm bracelet 14k / 18k charms 50 dwt	550	800	1000
Hinged plain 14k 5 dwts	50	75	100
Hinged plain 18k 5 dwts	75	100	125
Hinged plain 14k 10 dwts	100	150	175
Hinged plain 18k 10 dwts	140	200	225
Hinged two tone 18k 10 dwts	165	250	300
Hinged fancy engraved 18k 10 dwts	165	250	300

BRACELETS WITH GEMSTONES

Bracelets in this category will be priced by combining the basic value the bracelet would have with no stones (such as the values listed above) with the value of the gemstones. Gemstone value should be based on size (weight), color, clarity, and the number of stones.The reader should keep in mind that pricing should remain flexible to allow for variations in the quality and quantity of gemstones.The following basic examples are quite "generic" as far as style.This was done so that comparative values can be easily seen.As a general rule, the bracelets with only five stones will be of the hinged or cuff variety and those listed as having fifteen stones would be link style bracelets. The value of the diamond bracelets listed are based on samples where the size mixture of the diamonds would be fairly consistent. Diamond examples with large center stones would be valued higher than the samples.

amethyst 14k five 5 mm amethysts 15 dwts	175	300	400
amethyst 14k fifteen 5 mm amethysts 15 dwts	275	500	600
aquamarine 14k fifteen 5 mm aquas 15 dwts	400	600	700
citrine 14k fifteen 5 mm citrines 15 dwts	275	450	550
diamond 14k .30 ct tw 15 dwts	175	300	400
diamond 14k .50 ct tw 15 dwts	225	400	500
diamond 14k .75 ct tw 15 dwts	300	500	600
diamond 14k 1.00 ct tw 15 dwts	375	600	700
diamond 14k 1.25 ct tw 15 dwts	450	700	800
diamond 14k 1.50 ct tw 15 dwts	525	800	900
diamond 14k 1.75 ct tw 15 dwts	600	900	1000
diamond 14k 2.00 ct tw 15 dwts	700	1000	1100
emerald 14k five 5 mm emeralds 15 dwts	500	700	800
emerald 14k fifteen 5 mm emeralds 15 dwts	650	1000	1200
garnet 14k fifteen 5 mm garnets 15 dwts	200	350	450
opal 14k five 5 mm cabs 15 dwts	200	300	400
opal 14k fifteen 5 mm cabs 15 dwts	300	500	600
peridot 14k fifteen 5 mm peridots 15 dwts	300	450	550
ruby 14k five 5mm rubies 15 dwts	500	700	800
ruby 14k fifteen 5 mm rubies 15 dwts	600	1000	1200
sapphire 14k five 5 mm sapphires 15 dwts	325	500	600
sapphire 14k fifteen 5 mm sapphires 15 dwts	500	700	800

BEAD STYLE BRACELETS

Bracelets in this category are judged by the size, condition, color, and uniformity of the beads. As a general rule, the larger diameter beads will have a higher value than small ones and multiple strands will be higher than singles. All examples listed will include a gold clasp.

NOTE--Pearl bracelets are listed in the Pearl section

amber medium natural shape	75	150	200
amber large natural shape	125	200	250
coral bead 6 mm single strand	75	150	200
coral bead 10 mm single strand	125	200	250
ivory bead 6 mm single strand	75	150	200
ivory bead 10 mm single strand	100	200	250
jade bead 6 mm single strand	175	300	400
jade bead 10 mm single strand	250	400	500
lapis lazuli 6 mm single strand	75	150	200
lapis lazuli 10 mm single strand	125	200	250
mixed stone (carnelian, quartz, goldstone)	75	200	300
scarab style medium size	125	200	250
scarab style large size	150	250	300
turquoise bead 6 mm single strand	100	200	250
turquoise bead 10 mm single strand	125	250	300

BRACELETS (NO GEMSTONES)

18k, "C" shaped,16 mm, 33 dwt
c.1940
400 700 800

14k woven rope design 30 dwt
c.1940
300 450 500

Tiffany 18k tubular link design c.1940's 20 dwt
(note premium added for Tiffany)   400 600 700

Fancy link 18k 17mm wide 12dwt c.1930
250 400 450

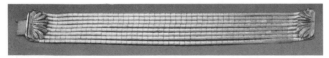

Eight strand 18k, 38 dwt, fancy end frames c. 1920
500 750 900

BRACELETS (NO GEMSTONES)

Rose and green 18k, 12 mm 43 dwt c.1930
700 1000 1200

Heavy two tone 18k rose and green 15 mm
wide 45 dwt c.1930   850 1100 1400

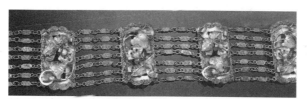

Multl color flower links Art Nouveau 18k c.1895
35 dwt   700 900 1100

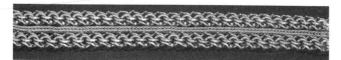

18k 21 mm wide multi strand 50 dwt c.1920
750 1200 1500

Five strand heavy 18k 30 mm wide 66 dwt c.1930
1000 1400 1800

BRACELETS (NO GEMSTONES)

18k lace style link Victorian 16 dwt c.1880
325 450 550

Half dome 18k, 35 dwt, c.1940   400 500 600

18k links with Mexican 22k gold pesos 57 dwt c.1945
1000   1500 1800

Charm bracelet 14k with 14 and 18k
charms 54 dwt c.1940   600 800   1000

BRACELETS (NO GEMSTONES)

Large charms 18k
bracelet 40 dwt,
c.1930 sm colored
stones ornament
the charms
600 800 900

18k, c.1930
florentine
design
33 dwt
450 600 700

Rare Victorian memorial- pierced to show inner
hair braids c.1880 18k 15 dwt
325 500 600 ☆

BRACELETS WITH GEMSTONES

Victorian with enamel 18k, 15 mm, one sm
ruby, eight rose cut diamonds, 27 dwt
 c.1870
700 1000 1500 ☆

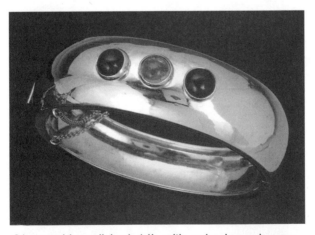

21 mm wide, polished, 14k, with cabochon ruby sapphire and emerald 22 dwt
c.1925
450 750 900

BRACELETS WITH GEMSTONES

ornate swirl top motif with
large cabochon emerald 18k
c.1925
1500 2250 2550 ☆

floral pierced design 18k,
12 emeralds 9 diamonds
(tw .90 ct) 14 dwt
 c.1935
500 750 850

22k, 7 mm engraved and
set with jade oval stones,
22 dwt
c.1915
500 800 1000

BRACELETS WITH GEMSTONES

platinum filigree with 2 pear emeralds (tw 4.5
ct) and diamonds (tw 1.5 ct) 20 mm
c.1910
3000 4500 5500 ☆☆

Pearl and Diamond (tw 1.9 ct) 14k wg filigree design sm
pearls 10 mm wide
c.1920
1450 2000 2500 ☆☆

BRACELETS WITH GEMSTONES

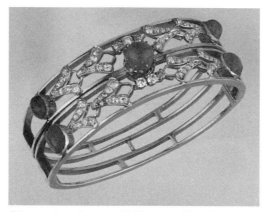

Diamond and emerald 25 mm wide 18k, open
work design with five cabochon emeralds, 2.0 ct
tw diamonds c.1910
1400 2200 2500

Amethyst (9x7 mm) with diamonds (38 diamonds 2.0 ct tw) c.1920
700 1000 1200

Diamond (5.0 ct tw) and sapphire linear bracelet, Art Deco
set in platinum c.1920   2500 4500 5000 ☆☆

Platinum filigree with diamonds(.95 ct tw) and small sapphires
c. 1910 Edwardian   500 800 1000

BRACELETS WITH GEMSTONES

Diamond and onyx Art Deco - (56 diamonds with 1.0 ct tw) platinum c.1920
2000 3000 3500 ☆☆·

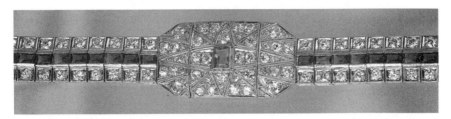

Diamond and emerald (95 diamonds with 6.25 ct tw) center line set with
emeralds, platinum c. 1910
4000 6000 7000 ☆☆☆

Diamond bracelet 7/16" wide 18k rose gold, 245 round diamonds with a
total weight of 17 cts. c.1910   8000 11,000 12,000 ☆☆☆

Art Deco sapphire and diamond line style - platinum 1/4" wide
180 sapphires, 26 diamonds (tw 5.0 ct) c.1925 3000 5000 6000
☆☆☆

BRACELETS WITH GEMSTONES

Diamond and sapphire, center 5.5 ct sapphire, 200 small diamonds
(tw 4.1 ct) 10mm wide platinum topped links with gold backs c.1935
2500 4000 4500 ⭐⭐

Diamond and sapphire line bracelet, c. 1950 Round platinum links with
18 diamonds (tw .90 ct) and 29 round sapphires   900 1500 1700

Diamond and platinum - linear style with 68 diamonds (tw 2.8 ct) c. 1930
1400 2000 2300 ⭐⭐

BEAD STYLE BRACELETS

Three strand Jade (5-9mm size) with gold clasp (sm diamond accents)
c. 1930   400 575 650

Coral bracelet four strand (7.5mm) gold and shell cameo clasp
c. 1925   325 450 500

Reminder, Pearl bracelets are listed in the pearl section.

CAMEOS

Rare large cameo-Victorian 3-3/4 by 2-3/4 inches, shell with 14k
frame, border of garnet beads c. 1870
600 900 1100 ☆☆☆

CAMEOS

The value of cameos and related jewelry pieces are influenced by several factors. The main factors to consider are quality of design and carvings, condition, material of the cameos, subject matter, age, size, frame material and other ornaments (pearl borders, enamel, diamonds, etc.) Cameo jewelry flourished during the Victorian period. Much of the subject matter was based upon Roman mythology with portraits of goddesses and allegorical scenes being the most popular. Individuals would also pose for the cameo artists in the early 19th century. Scenes and multi–figure cameos are generally priced higher than individual subjects, but the quality and condition of a piece will have a stronger influence on value than simply the subject matter.

Cameos are found most commonly carved from shell. Lava cameos coral cameos and hardstone cameos are more difficult to find. These are generally earlier pieces which will command a premium if the condition and quality are adequate. Other exotic stones which are carved as cameos include amethyst, opal, malachite, agate, turquoise, sapphire, emerald and ruby.

Filigree frames were also popular in the Victorian period. Finer frames with enamel or precious stone ornaments will add overall value to a cameo. Antique cameos are individually hand–carved creations. The collector should note that many contemporary cameos are now carved by ultrasound processes. This modern technology creates consistent designs and fine details, but the true artistic value is not present as it is with the expertly hand carved pieces.

BROOCHES: In this section, the small, medium and large designations will refer to the overall size of the cameo and frame. Small cameos are those which measure 1-1/2 " or less from top to bottom, medium cameos are 1-1/2" to 2" on the longest measurement and large cameos will measure over 2" from top to bottom. The entries refer to single subject cameos (one portrait usually in profile) unless the words "scene or unusual" appears in the description. Entries with scene or unusual designations refer to either double subject or unique portraits or to pastoral and other detailed carvings. The gf (gold filled) and 14k listings refer to the material of the frame the cameo is set in. The gf entries would also represent the value of a cameo in a gilt (gold on silver) or a simple silver frame. The 14k value levels can be varied slighty for 10k (somewhat less value) or 18k (higher value) frames. All listed prices are for cameos in near mint condition with no noticeable damage or chips.

shell small gf	40	75	100
shell medium gf	60	100	125
shell large gf	75	125	150
shell scene or unusual medium gf	90	200	250
shell scene or unusual large gf	125	225	275
shell small 14k	75	150	200
shell medium 14k	125	200	250
shell large 14k	175	250	300
shell scene or unusual medium 14k	250	350	400
shell scene or unusual large 14k	300	500	600
stone small gf	75	125	150
stone medium gf	100	150	200
stone large gf	125	200	250
stone scene or unusual medium gf	200	350	450
stone scene or unusual large gf	300	450	550
stone small 14k	175	250	300
stone medium 14k	300	450	600
stone large 14k	500	800	1200
stone scene or unusual medium 14k	400	600	800
stone scene or unusual large 14k	600	900	1500
lava small gf	100	200	250
lava medium gf	125	250	300
lava large gf	175	300	400
lava scene or unusual medium gf	300	500	600
lava small 14k	150	300	400
lava medium 14k	225	400	500

Brooches continued:

lava large 14k	350	600	700
lava scene or unusual medium 14k	400	600	700
lava scene or unusual large 14k	500	800	1000
amethyst small 14k	200	350	500
amethyst medium 14k	300	450	600
amethyst large 14k	400	600	800
coral small 14k	90	150	200
coral medium 14k	125	225	300
coral large 14k	200	325	450
ivory small 14k	200	300	400
ivory medium 14k	250	400	500
ivory large 14k	300	600	800
mother-of- pearl small 14k	100	150	200
mother-of-pearl medium 14k	125	175	225
mother-of-pearl large 14k	200	300	350
opal small 14k	200	400	500
opal medium 14k	300	500	600
opal large 14k	400	700	900
sapphire small 14k	800	1200	1400
sapphire medium 14k	1200	1800	2000
sapphire large 14k	2000	3000	3500

CAMEO RINGS (all in gold mounts)

shell	75	150	200
stone	150	250	300
lava	150	250	300
coral	75	150	200
tigers eye	75	150	200
opal	200	400	500

CAMEO EARRINGS (gold mounts)

shell	100	200	250
stone	200	400	500
lava	150	250	300
coral	125	200	275
ivory	150	250	350
opal	150	300	400

CAMEO STICKPINS (gold pins)

shell	50	100	125
stone	75	125	150
lava	75	150	200
coral	75	150	200
ivory	75	150	200
opal	100	175	225

CAMEO BRACELETS (all will be priced in gold frames with a minimum of five carved cameo frames in the bracelet)

shell	200	400	600
stone	400	800	1200
lava	400	800	1200
coral	200	400	600
ivory	300	600	800

CAMEO SUITES (three piece sets represent a brooch and a pair of earrings. A four piece set consists of a brooch, earrings and a ring.)

shell 3 pc suite	200	400	500
shell 4 pc suite	275	550	650
stone 3 pc suite	550	950	1250
stone 4 pc suite	700	1200	1500
coral 3 pc suite	300	450	550
coral 4 pc suite	400	650	850
ivory 3 pc suite	300	550	650
ivory 4 pc suite	400	800	1000
lava 3 pc suite	600	800	1000
lava 4 pc suite	900	1250	1500
opal 3 pc suite	800	1200	1500
opal 4 pc suite	950	1400	1800

CAMEO BROOCHES

Large shell-44x54mm-14kwg filigree frame mint c.1915
225 325 400

Victorian shell cameo14k rope frame-3 inches by 2 inches
c.1895
300 425 500

Shell cameo 43x53mm ornate frame 14k c.1920
225 325 400

Rare two figure cameo 54x63mm signed G.Noto, two lady and bird motif, 14k c.1950
600 850 950 ✩✩✩

Shell Greek Goddess 18k 2inches by 1-1/4 inch c.1900
200 350 450

Shell Greek Goddess 18k 2inches by 1-1/4 inch
c.1900
225 325 400

CAMEO BROOCHES

Shell Isadora Duncan
image,Art Nouveau
14k,2 inches by 1-1/4
c.1920
250 400 475 ☆☆

Shell fine detail, sterling
frame-2 by 1-3/4 inches
mint
c.1870
225 400 500

Shell three figures 18k
bezel mint-2-1/8 by 1-
3/4 inches
c.1880
225 300 450

Shell portrait of "Hebe"
14k frame 1-3/4 by 1-
1/2 inches-hinged lock-
et and glass on back
c.1880
250 400 500

CAMEO BROOCHES

Rare pastoral scene cameo,shell,14k filigree frame 3-3/4 by 3 inches highly detailed c.1890
500 975 1200 ☆☆

Georgian stone cameo, 17x20 mm c.1835
300 500 600 ☆☆·

Hardstone onyx cameo 33x39 mm, 18k c. 1900
350 550 650

Hardstone portrait, c.1890 14k bezel, 31x41mm
375 550 650

CAMEO BROOCHES

Hardstone portrait of a gentleman, 10k frame 30x38 mm c. 1885
450   550   650

Large hardstone Etruscan revival 18k frame, 2" by 1-3/4" c.1900
600 800 1000 ☆☆

Hardstone Lady's profile-superior quality 2" by 1-1/2" c. 189018k frame
1200 1500 2000 ☆☆

Sardonyx portrait first quality, 18k and pearl frame, 2" by 1-3/4"
c.1890
1200 1500 2000 ☆☆

CAMEO BROOCHES

Lava cameo 1-3/4" by 1-1/4 plain frame
c.1885
150 275 325

Lava 18k frame ladies portrait 2" by 1-1/2"
c.1875
200 325 375

Large portrait high relief 18k fancy frame 2-1/4 by 2" mint
c.1880
500 800 1000 ☆☆

Rare high relief scene (cherub and deer) 31x36mm 18k frame
c. 1875
350 550 650 ☆☆

CAMEO BROOCHES

Lava very high relief, girl and puppy motif 2" by 1-3/4" 14k
c. 1900
450 650 800 ☆☆☆

Rare natural sapphire cameo- ornate 18k frame, 1-3/4" by 1-1/2" high relief profile of an emperor
c.1880
2000 3000 3750 ☆☆☆☆

Amethyst cameo 1-3/4" by 1-3/8" gilt bezel woman with lyre motif
c. 1870

250 400 500 ☆☆

Opal cameo on onyx 18k frame 31x33 mm with 18k neck chain
c. 1910
400 600 700

CAMEO BROOCHES

Ivory cameo with pearls
18k frame 1-3/4" by 1-1/2"
two ladies in profile
c.1880
275 400 500

Rare turquoise cameo with
enamel, diamond and emer-
ald frame, 2-3/4" by 1-1/2"
25 rose cut diamonds, drop
at bottom of frame with small
emerald
 c.1900
600 850 1000 ☆☆☆

CAMEO RINGS

Hardstone ring
gents Roman pro-
file 14k mint
c. 1885
150 250 350

Hardstone ring with
enamel border and
pearls
c.1890
250 450 550 ☆

Hardstone ring
gents Roman pro-
file 14k
c. 1885
150 250 350

Hardstone ring
Victorian 18k
c.1890
150 275 325

Opal and diamond 18k,
8 diamonds tw .25ct
c.1890
450 700 800 ☆☆

CAMEO EARRINGS,STICKPINS,AND SUITES

Coral earrings gold bezel set, scarce double style
c.1910
250 400 600

Stone cameo stickpin 10k wg frame
c.1900
75 150 225

Lava stickpin 14k, Victorian 25x18m
c.1890
100 200 275

Victorian 3 pc suite c. 1875 hardstone (onyx) gold frames with half pearl borders, Mint
900 1200 1500 ☆☆☆

68

CUFFLINKS

Antique and vintage cufflinks are highly collectible The "mainstays" of jewelry for men were watches, rings and cufflinks. When evaluating cufflinks, be sure to look for sets in good condition. Since they were literally "worn on the cuff", many fine examples would become damaged through careless wear. Condition becomes very important on stone and gem set cufflinks.

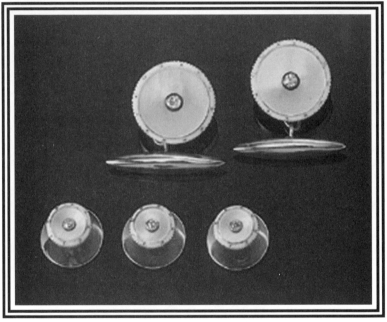

Mother-of-Pearl and diamond cuff and stud set,
18k, 14mm diameter 8 dwts c. 1910
350   600   750

CUFFLINKS

plain 14k 10 dwts	80	125	150
plain 18k 10 dwts	125	200	250
fancy engraved 14k 10 dwts	100	150	200
fancy engraved 18k 10 dwts	150	225	275
gold 18k with sm diamonds (tw .05-.10 ct)	175	300	400
platinum with sm diamonds (twt .05-.10 ct)	200	350	450
22k gold coin 10 dwts	225	350	400

Note: the following prices are for two stones with gold back pieces. For cuff sets with double stones (front and back-four stones total) the value doubles. All prices are for 14k gold mounts.

amethyst (two stones)	125	200	250
bloodstone	75	130	175
carnelian	100	200	300
coral	75	130	175
garnet	100	175	225
jade	150	300	400
lapis lazuli	75	150	175
malachite	75	150	175
moonstone	75	125	150
turquoise	75	125	150

CUFFLINKS

Gold button style
16mm with small
diamonds (.45 ct tw)
18k
c.1910
150 300 350

Ruby and diamond
(tw .10ct) oval 18k
11x16mm
c.1900
200 300 400

Gold coin set,
22k English 1/2
sovereigns
engraved 18k
oval back
7.5dwt
c.1920
175 250 300

Art Deco platinum
with sm diamonds
(.10 ct tw) and small
sapphires on border
10.5mm 18k back
c. 1920
225 350 450 ☆

CUFFLINKS

Platinum with cabochon sap-phire at center, 13mm engraved edges
c.1930
275 400 500 ☆

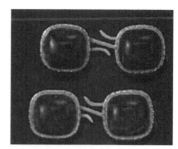

Lapis lazuli 11mm double cabochon 18k frames
c.1930
200 300 350

Carnelian double cabochon 14k frame 12mm
c.1910
200 300 400

Amethyst double cabochon 11.5mm 18k
c.1920
200 300 400

Victorian bird motif with coral beads, 18k
c.1880 17x51mm
350 550 750 ✩✩

EARRINGS

Period styles and characteristics are often very strongly represented in vintage earrings. Victorian, Nouveau, and Deco "looks" are good choices to collect. Earring settings listed will always be gold or platinum.The type of mounts will vary --wire or hoop style backs were most often used on Victorian period earrings while the later periods used posts and clip backs. Although the type of back used does not greatly affect the value of earrings, always look for originality and backs which are in good condition. Backs and mounts which have been poorly altered will diminish the value of the earrings. Due to the smaller size and lightweight nature of earrings, the value is not normally heavily related to the gold metal value. The design and period styling is very important in earrrings which only have a small amount of gems or stones. Beautiful workmanship and detailing can add a great deal to the value of gold earrings as evidenced by the highly collectible Victorian period examples. In earrings where the gems make up the majority of the design- the buyer should study the clarity, color, cut and total weight of the gems since this will be the underlying basis of value. This section will present earrings in the following order:

> Gold earrings plain or with small stones
> Colored gemstone earrings
> Diamond earrings and diamonds with emerald,
>   ruby and sapphire

EARRINGS GOLD

hoop plain 14k 3 dwts	25	50	75
hoop fancy 14k 3 dwts	40	60	90
button plain 14k 4 dwts	50	80	110
button fancy 14k 4 dwts	60	100	120
button with sm diamonds (.15-.25 ct tw)	125	175	225
filigree drop plain 14k 5 dwts	100	175	200
filigree with sm diamonds (.15-.25 ct tw)	150	250	300
flower form plain 18k	100	150	200
flower form fancy Nouveau 18k	100	200	300
Victorian ornate form 18k	200	350	450
Victorian ornate with sm stones	250	400	500

COLORED GEMSTONE EARRINGS

amber small	40	75	125
amber large	60	150	200
amethyst small	75	150	200
amethyst large	100	200	250
aquamarine small	100	175	200
aquamarine large	125	250	350
citrine small	100	175	225
citrine large	125	250	350
coral small	100	150	200
coral large	150	250	300
garnet small	50	100	150
garnet large	75	150	200
jade small	125	200	250
jade large	175	350	450
lapis lazuli small	75	125	175
lapis lazuli large	125	200	250
moonstone small	75	125	175
moonstone large	100	175	225
opal small	80	125	200
opal large	125	200	250
pearl	refer to the pearl section		
peridot small	75	150	200
peridot large	100	200	250
topaz small	75	150	200
topaz large	100	250	300
tourmaline small	125	200	250
tourmaline large	150	300	400
turquoise small	50	100	150
turquoise large	75	150	250

NOTE: The following sections will present earring prices and examples of earrings with diamonds, emeralds, rubies and sapphires. The listed prices are AVERAGES-they will represent an approximate value range. REMEMBER- the clarity, cut, and color of gems will have a bearing on the price an item will bring. The prices listed below are refective of the quality levels most commonly found in antique jewelry which is being sold in the current market. Premium grade gems, high end signed pieces and superior quality pieces can carry a much higher value.

DIAMOND EARRINGS

Note: Diamond solitares listed as tw .10 ct will be two well matched diamonds which are .05 ct each.

diamond solitare tw .20 ct	75	150	200
diamond solitare tw .30 ct	150	250	300
diamond solitare tw .40 ct	150	300	350
diamond solitare tw .50 ct	250	400	500
diamond solitare tw .60 ct	300	500	600
diamond solitare tw .75 ct	375	600	700
diamond solitare tw 1.00 ct	450	800	1000
diamond solitare tw 1.25 ct	600	1000	1200
diamond solitare tw 1.50 ct	1200	1800	2200
diamond solitare tw 2.00 ct	2000	3000	4000
multiple diamonds tw .25 ct	150	250	300
multiple diamonds tw .50 ct	250	450	600
multiple diamonds tw .75 ct	400	700	900
multiple diamonds tw 1.00 ct	600	1000	1200
multiple diamonds tw 1.50 ct	1100	1600	1800
multiple diamonds tw 2.00 ct	1300	2000	2400

EARRINGS GOLD

Victorian drop 18k 21x60 mm,
sm red stone and pearls
c.1880
300 400 600 ☆☆

Victorian pearl and sm
turquoise drops, 18k
c.1885
300 400 600 ☆☆

Art Nouveau 18k flower form w/ small
pearl 25x26 mm
c.1915
150 250 350

Art Nouveau "orchid" form
18k pearl center 14x25 mm
c.1915
150 250 350

EARRINGS GOLD

Victorian drop, pear
shape with half pearls
18k 14x33 mm
c.1885
300 400 500 ☆

White enamel on 18k
dangle with small
sapphire 11.5mm
long Victorian
c. 1885
250 350 450

Flower form 18k
18x25mm Art
Nouveau c. 1900
small pearl
150 250 350

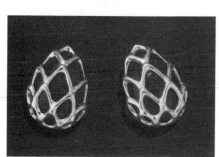

Enamel and 18k "strawberry"
motif20x26mm
signed "Tiffany"
c. 1940
400 600 800 ☆☆☆

*without Tiffany signature
175 275 350

EARRINGS GOLD

Victorian bird motif
with coral beads,
18k 17x51mm
c.1880
350 500 700 ☆☆

Round 18k 13mm with
sm rubies and diamonds
c.1925
150 300 400

Victorian 18k 15x33 mm,
pearl enamel and ruby
c. 1890
250 400 500

Platinum filigree and
diamonds , 11x37mm
set with two .02 ct
diamonds
c.1920
200 300 350

COLORED GEMSTONE EARRINGS

Coral round, 15mm 18k
with two .10 ct dia-
monds
c.1930
200 300 375

Tiffany four leaf clover
design, peridot, citrine,
amethyst, and a pink
sapphire,18k, sm diamond
at center
c.1950
500 750 900 ☆☆

Dangles with sm pearls and
tourmaline 18k, 52 mm long
c.1900
225 375 450

Coral 15mm diameter,
18k, white sapphire
accent stones
c.1930
200 300 375

COLORED GEMSTONE EARRINGS

Opals (15x 8
mm) with 18k
leaf form and
sm diamond
c.1940
125 175 250

Amethyst
(12x9 mm)
six diamonds
(tw .60 ct)
18k
c. 1910
200 300 375

PRECIOUS GEMSTONE EARRINGS

Sapphire and diamonds
32 sm diamonds (tw
1.1ct) pear shaped
sapphires, plat/18k
mounts
c.1910
500 700 800

Victorian diamond
drops, cushion cuts,
one1.5 ct the other
1.3 ct, 2.8 ct tw, H
color, SI3/Vs1
c.1890
3000 4500 6000 ☆☆

Diamond and platinum
European cuts, upper
diamonds are .70 ct
each , lower diamonds
are 1.9 ct each   (tw
5.20 ct) K/SI 2
c.1900
5500 8000 10000 ☆☆☆

Amethyst and dia-
mond Art Deco dan-
gles, 24mm long,
platinum, faceted
amethyst stones,
round diamonds (tw
.60 ct)
c.1925
500 900 1200

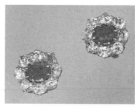

Emerald and diamond,
oval emeralds 5x4mm,
16 diamonds total
(tw 1.0 ct) 18k
 c.1895
700 950 1200 ☆☆

Ruby, sapphire and diamond, 25x26mm, wg clips with sm cabochon rubies and sapphires, sm diamonds
c.1940
400 600 700

Diamond and wg drops 18k, 32mm long, Art Deco tw.45 ct,
c.1920
300 500 600

Diamond pear shapes tw .75ct plat
c.1910
400 550 650

Emerald and Diamond 45mm long, two 4 carat pear shaped emeralds, 36 round diamonds (tw 2.1ct) platinum
c.1930
4500 6500 7500 ☆☆☆

Diamond 18k tw .65ct Victorian
c.1890
300 500 600

PRECIOUS GEMSTONE EARRINGS

Diamond and
garnets 18k tw
1.0 ct 11mm
c.1920
600 800 900

Diamond platinum tw
.50 ct Victorian c.1890
300 500 600

Diamond dangles
tw .30 ct plat and
18k, 36 mm long
c.1920
250 375 500

Victorian diamond
and 18k, center pear
shaped dia. five outer
rounds, tw 1.4 ct
c.1900
800 1200 1500 ☆

Victorian diamond and
18k, 20 rose cut dia-
monds, tw .80 ct
11x17mm c.1895
400 600 700

Diamonds in
snowflake motif 18k
and plat. 18 dia-
monds tw .50 ct
c.1915
300 450 550

Diamond row style
drops,14 diamonds
tw2.0ct. 18k mount
c. 1920
1400 1800 2200

Edwardian diamond and
sapphire-total diamond
weight 3.3 cts. central
faceted sapphires
(3.5x5mm) overall
43 mm x 21 mm
c.1910
1400 2200 2500 ☆☆

84

PRECIOUS GEMSTONE EARRINGS

Filigree style drops,
platinum 35mm long
with 20 small single cut
diamonds (tw .25 ct)
c.1915
175 275 375

Victorian flower
and diamond
25mm long, plat-
inum with 20 dia-
monds (tw .70ct)
c.1900
350 500 600

Rose gold and
diamond
Victorian 18k,
16mm with sm
diamonds
(tw .60 ct)
c.1885
400 500 600

Diamond dangles 18k
wg 21mm long, four
diamonds tw .50 ct
c.1930
300 500 600

Victorian earrings
17 mm long, rose and
cushion cut diamonds
(tw .40 ct) 18k
c.1890
300 550 650 ☆

Flower motif 18k 11mm
with eight diamonds on
each earring
(tw .55ct) c.1905
300 500 600

PRECIOUS GEMSTONE EARRINGS

Diamond drops 9 diamonds on each piece (tw .60 ct) platinum tops 18k backs c.1920 11mm long c.1920
450 600 750 ☆

Diamond button style-two.10 ct round diamonds with outer border of blue enamel, 18k, 9mm
c.1910
250 350 450

Victorian, rose cut diamonds (tw .60 ct) 14k floral mount 12mm wide c.1885
200 300 350

Diamond and sapphire drops, 18k 28mm long , oval cab sapphires,small rose diamonds (tw .50 ct) c.1890
500 750 850 ☆

Sapphire and diamonds, platinum 12x18mm, center row of four diamonds (tw .16 ct) triangular sapphires
c.1915
300 450 550

Art Deco diamond and onyx, 30mm long, sm diamonds tw .50 ct 18k and plat. c.1920
400 600 700 ☆

BASIC ENAMEL TECHNIQUES

Enameling can add interest and color to many jewelry forms—it is used as either an accent on frames and mounts or it may actually be the center-piece or primary focal point of a design. There are six basic enamel techniques.

Enamel, gold and pearl dragonfly pin. Cloisonne enameled wings in blue, red, green and yellows, Pearl mid-section, black enamel head with ruby eyes, 18k 46x54 mm c.1920
500 700 1000 ☆

CLOISONNE: A design is formed by thin metal strips which are soldered to the background piece. The metal strips are then divided into smaller "cells" by other metal strips. The cells are filled or "packed" with the enamel and then fired.

CHAMPLEVE: This method is similar to cloisonne, except the "cells" or divisions which hold the enamels are actually cut into the main metal background. The recesses are often undercut and the enamel is then applied and fired. Casting or stamping techniques are also used to form the "cells" or "recesses" for the champleve enamel.

Magnificent enamel, gold and diamond brooch. Bird of Paradise design, 18k 2-3/4"x4" round diamonds ornament the wings (tw 2.5 ct). The feather areas are engraved and colored with blue, red, green and yellow hues of bassetaille translucent enamel. c.1915
2000 4000 5000 ☆☆☆

BASIC ENAMEL TECHNIQUES

BASSETAILLE: In this form of enameling, the main metal piece is engraved or chased with a design or pattern. Then, a series of transparent or translucent enamels are applied over the engraved surface. This technique was popular to form sunburst, ripple or engine–turned effects.This style is also refered to as "guilloche" enameling.

PLIQUE–A–JOUR: This enamel process is often considered the most difficult and yet the most beautiful when done by an expert. A stained–glass window effect is produced by forming filigree cells or frames from metal. These cells are then undercut and placed on a mica surface. The enamel is filled and fired several times and the temporary back piece (the mica) is removed and the enamel is polished. The transparent colors or "windows" which are produced by plique a jour enameling were the basis for many spectacular jewelry pieces of the Art Nouveau period.

Enameled portrait of a lady, French Limoges, 18k frame set with twenty diamonds (tw 4.0 ct) 2"x1-3/4" pink, aqua, gold and cobalt blue colors, c.1900
1200 1850 2000 ☆ ☆

PAINTED ENAMEL: Painted enamel is done on the surface of the metal plate without the use of cells or engraved channels. A "base coat" of white or clear enamel is first applied and fired. Then other colors are painted and blended on top. The colors are built up separately and the piece is then re–fired at a lower temperature than that which was used for the base enamel. This process eliminates "run on" or smearing of the colors. The finishing step is the application of a clear transparent enamel. Limoges is a popular form of painted enamel.

NIELLO: This black shade of enameling is produced by combining silver, copper and lead. The mixture is melted and an amalgam is formed by adding sulphur. The fine powder produced is then applied and fired onto the piece which is being decorated. After several applications and polishing, the result is a smooth, rich black finish which often forms the background to an engraved silver or gold scene. The art of niello enameling is scarce. Some of the finest examples of this art are found on silver pocket watches produced during the early 1900's.

Watch fob Niello on silver c. 1910   100 200 275

Three scarce Niello pocket watches. Niello on silver c. 1910
175 325 425

ENAMEL PRICE LEVELS

This section will show many fine examples of enamel enhanced jewelry with current price levels. The variables which are found in the enameled pieces make general pricing difficult at best. Each piece can vary as far as condition, design, color and type of enamel technique used. The reader should approach each enamel piece separately and compare the piece to other similar examples which are priced in this book. Good quality enamel decoration will generally increase an objects value by at least 75% and the value can easily go higher for better quality pieces. When appraising an enameled piece, it is best to establish a base price the item would have if enamel was not a part of the design. Then add to that value based upon the quality, quantity, condition and design of the enamel. Also keep in mind that the better enamel items are "enamel on gold"- enamel on silver is generally not as expensive. The exception to this would be the finer niello enamel pieces where the contrast between the soft white of the silver and the black of the niello was used to create beautifully detailed scenes. Enameled scenes and portraits which are finely colored and shaded will bring higher values than single color "pattern" enamels or pieces with simple enameled accents.

The value of enameled jewelry is based on several factors--- quality of the enamel work, design, the style or period depicted (Art nouveau, Art Deco etc.) and most importantly the condition. Damaged enameled pieces will suffer a great loss of value since high quality restoration work is both difficult to find and expensive. Repaired enamels are often found with soft enamel in place of the original hard ename, this type of work will also lower the value. In general, enameling on gold will bring a higher value than a similar piece which is enamel on silver. Polychrome portrait enamels and scenes will bring a higher value than single color patterns and pieces which only have enameled accent lines or borders. The following examples are all in good condition with no major repairs or damage. Enameled jewelry is highly collectible. The addition of color can bring a design to life and add to the charm and eye appeal of the item. Painted ivory, reverse glass paintings, and porcelain miniatures are other forms of colorful jewelry.

ENAMEL BRACELETS

Art Deco bracelet, 18k with black, red, and grey enameled links round carnelian and onyx links c. 1920   750 1100 1500 ✫✫

Gold and enamel Victorian bracelet 18k, 15mm wide blue and white enamel, rose diamonds
c.1880
575 900 1100 ✫✫

ENAMEL EARRINGS

Earrings with white enamel, 18k long dangles Victorian
c.1880
200 350 450

Tiffany enameled strawberry earrings, 18k, 20x26mm c.1930
400 600 800 ✫✫

ENAMEL PENDANTS

Enameled locket with fine colored portrait, 18k with gold neck chain, 2" diameter
c.1880
600 1000 1200 ☆☆

Pendant with "La Virgin de Lourdes" polychrome scene 18k frame 36mm
c.1915
300 400 500 ☆·

Pendant, 18k with red white and blue enamel 34mm, central mine cut diamond
c.1910
125 250 350

Painted portrait, fine detail, 18k frame 25x39mm, with 18k neck chain
c.1925
300 500 600 ☆

ENAMEL PINS/BROOCHES

Victorian enamel and
pearl, 18k 32x39 mm,
blue and multicolor
enamel flowers, small
rubies,
c.1880
400 600 700 ☆

Peacock pin, cloisonne
enamel at center,18k
41x45mm colored gem-
stones on the feather
ends
c.1930
350 600 700 ☆

Boy and dog pin, 14k with
red and blue enamel on
cap, 23x53mm
c.1910
300 500 600 ☆

Victorian enamel and pearl
pin, 18k 30mm, black
enamel striped design
c.1885
200 350 450

ENAMEL PINS/BROOCHES

Enameled beetle
pin, 18k 20x30mm
red enamel body
with small
diamonds
c.1910
300 500 600

Pansy pin, 18k white and
blue enamel, small dia-
mond 30mm
c.1920
300 450 550

Victorian pin with black enamel,
pearls and turquoise 18k,
40x50mm
c.1880
300 500 600

ENAMEL RINGS

Enamel is rarely found on rings--antique examples in good condition are highly collectible and scarce. The factors behind this scarcity are simply that rings were made for wearing on the finger-therefore exposing any exterior decoration such as enamel to damage. Also, rings needed to have the capacity to be sized and any enamel on a ring band or shank would be easily damaged by bending or cutting the shank. A few examples of interesting enamel rings are shown below..

Cartier "cigar" band ring, 18k, champleve red enamel in recessed areas, gold lettering and "Habana corona" design ring is signed and numbered limited production
c.1920
900 1400 1600 ☆ ☆

Enamel and diamond ring, 18k large (33x19mm) blue background enamel, diamond pattern on top (tw .85 ct)
c. 1890
1000 1500 1750 ☆

ENAMEL STICKPINS

Enameled stickpins are very desirable in the collectors market. Due to the small surface space usually found on the pins , the enamel techniques are more difficult to produce. Choice examples of enamel "in miniature" are quite rare and the superior pieces will command a premium.

Rare Art Nouveau stickpin, enameled facial tones, with expertly detailed features and natural colors, 18k gold, sm diamond ruby and emerald hair ornaments
c.1925
500 850 1000 ☆☆

Three flower enameled pin, 18k lavender, white and purple hues, small diamond at center
c.1915
300 500 600 ☆

Egyptian revival period stickpin, 18k enameled pharoh profile blue, green and reds
c.1925
300 450 650 ☆

ENAMEL WATCHES

Watch cases have always been one of the most popular areas for enamel artists to display their craft. The relatively flat surfaces and the generous size of watch cases allowed for the creation of detailed portraits, scenes and designs. Enameled watches also mirror the characteristics of the various jewelry periods very well. This section will highlight the most widely seen styles of enameled watches and identify the periods which they represent. More examples and detailed pricing will be found in the watch section of this book.

Swiss enamel on silver Art Nouveau, openface, with silver neck chain
c.1930
250 450 550

Swiss enamel on silver, late Victorian, openface with matching pin
c.1890
200 350 450

Swiss enamel on 18k, Art nouveau, hunters case
c.1920
400 700 800

Swiss enamel on silver detailed scene with fleur-de-lis pin, openface Victorian
c.1890
500 600 700 ☆

ENAMEL WATCHES

Swiss enamel on silver with chain, pearl border and fine scene, openface Victorian
c.1885
400 700 800 ☆

Miniature enamel "Joan of Arc" watch 18k hunter case Swiss, 24mm, rose diamonds on headband, fine quality
c.1890
700 1100 1300

Enameled keywind watch, Swiss early Victorian 18k with colorful garden scene, openface 30mm
c.1870
400 600 700 ☆

Swiss18k wristwatch with black enamel Victorian line style patterns, 4 small diamonds 24mm
c.1905
250 400 500

Lady's enameled bezel wristwatch, Swiss, 18k black green red and blue Art Deco design, 14x20mm
c.1920
300 450 550 ☆

NECKLACES

A distinction must be made between "necklaces" and neck chains which are combined with a drop or pendant. Simple neck chains are designed to carry a charm or enhancer but a necklace can easily stand on its own as a jewelry piece. The necklace section will list values in the following order: gold link style (no gemstones), colored gemstone and bead styles, and finally diamond necklaces.

GOLD LINK

round, curb, or oval link 14k 10 dwts	90	150	200
round, curb, or oval link 18k 10 dwts	130	200	250
mesh or filigree links 14k 10 dwts	100	175	225
mesh or filigree links 18k 10 dwts	150	225	275
engraved fancy panel link 14k 10 dwts	125	200	250
engraved fancy panel link 18k 10 dwts	175	250	300

BEAD AND COLORED STONE NECKLACES

Note: values in this category are based on a standard length of approximately 18 to 25 inches and on a typical bead diameter of 6 to 8 millimeters. Prices are also based on single strands-adjust values for variations. In general, the longer strands and larger diameter beads will bring higher prices than short strands or small beads.

Amber	50	100	200
Amethyst	100	250	350
Aquamarine	250	500	700
Citrine	200	400	500
Coral	100	200	300
Garnet	100	175	250
Jade	200	400	500
Lapis Lazuli	75	150	225
Moonstone	100	200	300
Opal	200	400	500
Pearls	refer to pearl section		
Peridot	150	300	400
Topaz	100	200	300
Tourmaline	200	400	500
Turquoise	100	200	275

NECKLACES

DIAMOND NECKLACES: Antique diamond necklaces are quite scarce and highly sought after by collectors of jewelry. The high ruffled collar designs of Victorian period fashions were not well suited for the wearing of diamond necklaces. The Edwardian and Belle Epoque periods (1890-1915) saw a change in ladies fashion with lower necklines which highlighted the neck and chest. Jewelers began to produce more elaborate floral or garland style necklaces with numerous mine cut diamonds set in elegant platinum mounts. All examples of this style are very collectible and general pricing information will be given. Values are roughly based on the total diamond weight a piece has, but variables such as diamond clarity, cut and color must also be considered. Designs with a strong eye appeal and pieces which are expertly made will be valued at a higher rate than those which tend to be "heavier " in the metal work and settings. The premier diamond necklaces as well as diamonds combined with rubies, emeralds, or sapphires are very rare. Individual pieces should be priced and appraised base on the rarity, quality and quantity of the gemstones, and the overall workmanship and design.

Diamond tw .50 ct	250	500	650
Diamond tw .75 ct	400	750	900
Diamond tw 1.00 ct	500	900	1200
Diamond tw 1.50 ct	750	1350	1750
Diamond tw 2.00 ct	1100	1800	2300
Diamond tw 2.50 ct	1500	2250	2850
Diamond tw 3.00 ct	1800	2700	3500
Diamond tw 3.50 ct	2300	3250	4000
Diamond tw 4.00 ct	2700	4000	5000
Diamond tw 5.00 ct	3300	6000	7000

GOLD LINK NECKLACES

Fancy link necklace, pierced clover design, 14k 56" 15 dwt c.1925
300 450 600

Gold necklace, 18k 40" fancy links 15 dwt c.1915   350 500 675

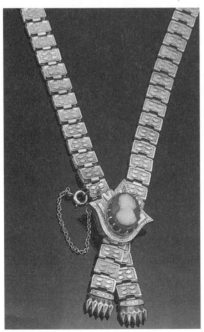

Victorian necklace with small cameo, 14k engraved panel style links, hardstone cameo 28", 17dwt, c.1880
350 550 650 ☆

GOLD LINK NECKLACES

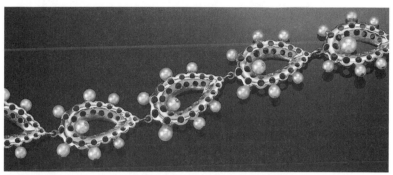

Gold and pearls 14k teardrop links with pearls 15" 20 dwt c.1930
225 400 500

Gold snake necklace, 18k 15" long, gold mesh combined with fine
detailed snake heads, ruby eyes, Egyptian revival influence,75 dwt
c.1930
1500 2500 3000 ✩✩

COLORED STONE NECKLACES

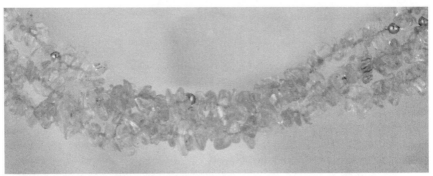

Triple strand aquamarine, natural polished stones with gold bead spacers
22" long, approx 650 carats of aquamarine
c.1915
500 1000 1200 ☆

Rare coral necklace, with superior carved fire coral centerpiece and clasp 19" long, triple strand, centerpiece carved with birds, leaves, flowers, 18k gold back frame
c.1930
550 1000 1250 ☆

COLORED STONE NECKLACES

Natural garnet bead necklace, 4-6 mm size, 18" long, 18k clasp with pearls c.1920
350 600 700

DIAMOND NECKLACE

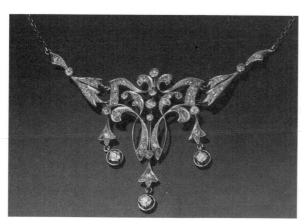

Diamond garland style, 49 diamonds, tw 2.0 ct platinum,18" length, Belle epoque period c.1910
1000 1800 2400 ☆☆

A GUIDE TO PEARLS, VALUES, TYPES AND CONDITION

The pearl is a splendid gem which has been used to create fine jewelry for thousands of years. Saltwater oysters and freshwater mollusks naturally produce pearls. When an outside object enters and irritates the interior, a "nacre" is secreted to blanket the irritant. As the nacre layers build up, the pearl forms. Cultured pearls are produced by an outside (non–natural) introduction of a seed or irritant. In general, cultured pearls will have a thinner coating of nacre than natural pearls.

The thickness of nacre is directly related to the luster a pearl will exhibit. "Luster" is the term used to describe the reflective characteristics of a pearl. Pearls with high luster will have a liveliness to the iridescent play of light. The reflective images from a low luster pearl will be much more subdued and "flatter" or less lively.

The collector should always consider the "luster" of a pearl as the most important quality. In making judgements regarding luster, it is best to compare more than one strand side by side. Look for both the light "glow" or reflective properties as well as the underlying iridescent play of colors and light.

The other variables to consider when evaluating pearls are size, color, condition and the shape or type.

SIZE

The diameter of round pearls are listed in millimeters. In general, the larger the diameter, the more valuable the pearl. Round pearls larger than 9 millimeters (mm) are quite scarce and they command a premium.

Odd shaped pearls are measured in millimeters for both the length and width. Natural pearls are also weighed in grains—four grains equal one carat. Uniformity of size is important in pearl necklaces and bracelets. Graduated strands should also be viewed for symmetry of size.

ROUND MILLIMETER SIZES

SHAPE & TYPE

BAROQUE: an irregular shape, non–symmetrical pearl. These are generally less valuable than large round pearls, yet they are used in jewelry due to their interesting shapes and the "play" of colors they produce.

HALF PEARL: generally small pearls which are used as border or edge decorations. Popular as outer frame accents on cameos and enameled pendant watches. Half pearls are sometimes incorrectly referred to as "seed pearls". Seed pearls are actually tiny round pearls which are drilled and strung to form outer borders.

THREE–QUARTER: these are round pearls which have one end cut off—the part which is removed is usually a blemished area. Pearls of this type are found in recessed "cup–style" settings and often used in earrings. The value is considerably less than that of a full round of equal size.

BIWA or FRESHWATER PEARLS: irregular pearls with a long, narrow shape and irregular surfaces. These appear in many colors. The freshwater varieties are relatively plentiful and common. Multi–strand necklaces are often formed from this type of pearl.

BLISTER and MABE: cultured, blister pearls area dome–shaped variety which grows attached to a mollusk's outer shell. When they are cut off, one side remains flat with no coating of nacre. Mabe pearls have a similar shape, yet they are less valuable. Mabe pearls are produced when a hollow, blister pearl is removed from the interior of an oyster. This thin blister is then filled with epoxy and combined with an added backing of mother of pearl.

SOUTH SEA PEARLS: these large, cultured pearls are considered to be some of the finest produced. The size is generally large (10–15 mm) and they appear in both pinkish–white and a white with soft silver overtones. The large amount of nacre and resulting high luster make these pearls very desirable.

COLOR

Pearls appear in a wide variety of colors. White is the main color encountered, yet shades of silver, pink, black and grey are also popular. The color a pearl shows is a secondary factor when determining value—the luster is generally considered to be of greater importance. The color evaluation process should take the following factors into consideration: 1) The basic body color; 2) The secondary overtones or color tints which are present; 3) The play of multi–hued "rainbow" effects or iridescence.

NOTE: Many black, grey and other colored pearls are dyed and not natural.

CONDITION

The surface or "outer skin" of a pearl will frequently have natural imperfections or slight blemishes. Minor imperfections will not significantly devalue a pearl if they are small in number and relatively inconspicuous. Heavy pitting, bumps, cracks and welts will bring the value down, especially when these flaws are easily seen by the naked eye. Pearls with major loss of nacre are also problems and they may be unsalable.

PEARL CARE AND CLEANING

Pearls are a soft gem and they must be handled with care.cleaning solvents and ultrasonic cleaners should not be used. Make–up, perfume, hair spray and body oils can be detrimental to a pearl's surface. A mild soapy water can be used to clean pearls and they should be wiped clean with a soft cloth after being worn.

PEARLS
GENERAL PRICES

BRACELETS

Pearl bracelets are valued based on the size of the pearls, the number of strands, and the quality. Clasps can add significant value when they are set with precious gemstones and diamonds. Since adding to the length of a bracelet can be a difficult procedure- always check that the length is sufficient to wear.

NOTE-values listed below reflect bracelets with simple gold clasps- add value for gemstone enhanced varieties.

single strand small seed pearls	30	60	80
single strand freshwater	40	80	100
single strand round cultured 3-4 mm	35	70	100
single strand round cultured 5 mm	50	100	130
single strand round cultured 6-7 mm	90	150	175
single strand round cultured 7.5-8 mm	120	175	250
single strand round cultured 8.5-9 mm	200	400	550

The following multi strand examples will have a minimum of four strands

multi strand small seed pearls	75	125	200
multi strand freshwater	75	125	200
multi strand cultured 3-4 mm	125	200	275
multi strand cultured 5 mm	175	300	400
multi strand cultured 6-7 mm	250	400	500
multi strand cultured 7.5-8 mm	350	550	650
mutli strand cultured 8.5-9 mm	400	800	900

PEARL EARRINGS

single cultured 3-4 mm	20	40	60
single cultured 4.5-5.5 mm	35	70	90
single cultured 6-7 mm	50	90	120
single cultured 7.5-8.5 mm	75	130	175
single cultured 9-10 mm	150	300	400
five pearl clusters 3-6 mm pearls	75	150	200
five pearl clusters 6-8 mm pearls	100	200	225
five pearl clusters 8 mm pearls	150	225	300
single South Seas pearls 9-10 mm	600	1000	1300
single South Seas pearls 11-plus mm	1000	1500	2000

PEARL NECKLACES

In this category the size luster, quality and number of pearls are the main factors which must be taken into account. The uniformity of size, color and luster is also important to consider as well as the fineness and match of sizes which make up graduated necklaces. Styles will be priced with standard gold barrel or filigree clasps.

Necklaces with better diamond or other gemstone set clasps will carry additional value. Many pearl necklaces are also combined with gemstone enhancers. The enhancer values should be considered as a separate part of the pricing. The following prices are for single strands--multiple strands will increase the values times the number of strands.

STANDARD PEARL NECKLACE LENGTHS

Choker	14–16"
Princess	18"
Matinee	20–24"
Opera	28–32"
Rope	40–45"
Lariat	48" and longer

freshwater choker length	50	90	110
freshwater matinee length	65	110	125
freshwater opera length	80	125	150
cultured 3-6mm graduated choker	75	125	175
cultured 5-8mm graduated choker	100	150	200
cultured 7-10mm graduated choker	150	225	300
cultured 3-6mm graduated matinee	100	175	200
cultured 7-10mm graduated matinee	150	250	300
cultured 3mm choker	50	100	125
cultuerd 5mm choker	75	125	200
cultured 7mm choker	100	175	225
cultured 9mm choker	600	1000	1500
cultured 3mm matinee	75	125	150
cultured 5mm matinee	100	175	225
cultured 7mm matinee	200	400	600
cultured 9mm matinee	800	1500	2200
cultured 3mm opera	125	200	250
cultured 5mm opera	150	250	350
cultured 7mm opera	300	500	700
cultured 9mm opera	1200	2000	3000
South Seas 10mm plus--choker	RARE		
South Seas 10mm plus--matinee	RARE		
South Seas 10mm plus--opera	RARE		

PEARL PENDANTS AND BROOCHES: Pearls are not typically found as the main focal point or primary center of value on pins and brooches. They were used more as accent decorations and as frame ornaments. The exception would be larger pearls and rare South Seas pearls which are displayed as pendant drops.

PEARL RINGS: follow a similar pattern--many smaller pearls will serve as side decorations while the large and rare pearls are found as the main centerpiece stone on the high valued rings. Examples of both common and rare pendants, brooches and rings will follow.

PEARL BRACELETS

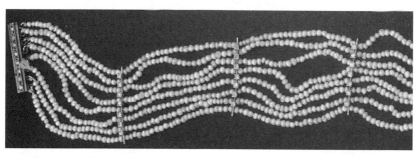

seed pearl multi-strand, eight strands, 14k wg clasp and spacer bars, small diamond accents (tw .40 ct) c.1920   200 325 400

Pearl and diamonds, five strand 8.5 mm pearls, 18k spacer bars set with diamonds, large star motif clasp with diamonds (tw 1.35 ct) c1940
1000 1500 1800 ☆

PEARL EARRINGS

Single cultured pearl
4mm, frame of small
diamonds (tw .60 ct)
18k c.1900
300 450 550

Victorian drops with
seed and natural
pearls, 19x63 mm
overall size,
18k filigree and wire
frames, c.1880
400 700 900 ☆

Platinum diamond and
pearls, 13x15 mm
south seas pearls with
exceptional luster, plat-
inum tops with many
diamonds (tw 1.50 ct)
c.1920
1500 3000 4000 ☆☆

Dangle earrings,
three 5 mm pearls
and one .15ct dia-
mond on each drop
18k c.1900
250 400 500

Natural black south seas
pearl earrings, first quality
pearls 11.5 mm in diameter,
14k mounts with diamond
borders (tw .80 ct) c.1950
600 1100 1300 ☆

South seas pearl
and diamond
drops, 14x15mm
pearls, linear plat-
inum drops with
eight diamonds
each (tw 1.1 ct)
c.1930
1500 3000 4000
☆☆

PEARL NECKLACES

Matinee 5mm cultured 25" with gold disc enhancer (sm dia monds) c.1930
250 400 500

Matinee 5.5mm cultured 24" with smoky topaz and 18k enhancer c.1940
300 450 550

Five strand choker, 4 mm pearls 13" long with 18k and coral flower enhancer c.1930
700 1200 1400

PEARL NECKLACES

Seven strand princess length 18", 5mm pearls well matched, 18k Deco
style clasp with rubies and diamonds (tw .50ct)   2500 3500 4000 ☆☆

Single strand, cultured 7mm 20" matinee c.1930
200 350 450

PEARL NECKLACES

Five strand, 6 mm, with platinum and diamond clasp, 32 " long, total diamond weight 5.00 ct. c. 1930   2750   4500   5000 ☆☆

STANDARD PEARL NECKLACE LENGTHS

Choker	14–16"
Princess	18"
Matinee	20–24"
Opera	28–32"
Rope	40–45"
Lariat	48" and longer

PEARL PINS & PENDANTS

Art Nouveau pin 18k and pearls,
35x70 mm, 9 dwt c.1915
200 375 450

Pearl, diamond and ruby brooch,
double row of half pearls, rose
cut diamonds (tw 1.0 ct), cabochon rubies, 18k, 30x37 mm
Victorian c.1870
1000 1550 1750 ☆

Large south
seas pearl
11x15 mm ,
platinum top
with .50 ct tw
diamonds,
platinum chain,
c.1925
1000 1500 1850 ☆

Victorian pin, baroque pearls, 18k
bar and chain links, two sm diamonds   c.1890
150 275 325

Pearl star motif, numerous half
pearls, central.05 ct diamond
25mm 14k c.1930
150 225 300

PEARL RINGS

Natural black pearl ring, 18k outer diamonds (tw .40 ct) central 11.5mm natural black pearl c.1940
500 800 900

South Seas 15.5 mm natural black pearl, 18k, diamond frame (tw .60 ct) c.1950
2250 3500 4000 ☆☆

Pearl and diamonds 18k, two 4 mm pearls, six diamonds (tw .20 ct) c.1900
150 225 300

Pearl and diamonds (tw .20 ct), six 3.5 mm pearls, 18k fan motif o.1920
150 300 400

Important large baroque pearl, 16x18x21 mm, 18k with tw .20 ct diamonds , rare size, first quality luster, color and condition c.1950
5000 7500 8500 ☆☆☆

Large mobe pearl, 16mm across, 18k with sm side diamonds (tw .30 ct) c.1940
200 350 450

Pearl ring, 18k with sm diamonds (tw .25 ct) set between nine 6 mm pearls, checkerboard motif c.1930
150 300 400

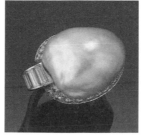

Important large natural baroque pearl, 17x20 mm, platinum setting with round and baguette diamonds (tw 2.5 ct) c.1930
2500 5000 6000 ☆☆

PENDANTS

Pendants are generally lighter and more delicate than brooches or pins and they are designed to be worn on a neck chain. Pendant jewelry became very popular in the early 1900's as the fashions changed to a more open neckline style. Pendants are also refered to as lavalieres. The Art Nouveau, Edwardian and Belle Epoque periods are strongly represented by the styling of many beautiful and highly collectible pendants. Prices listed will also include a light or medium-light weight gold neck chain. Very fancy chains would add additional value.

GOLD PENDANTS (no gemstones)

plain 14k 5dwts	45	75	100
plain 18k 5dwts	65	100	125
locket square 14k 5 dwts	65	125	150
heart shaped locket 14k 5 dwts	75	125	150
memorial locket oval 18k 5 dwts	100	175	225
Nouveau style raised relief portrait 18k 5 dwts	125	200	250
locket with enamel accents 14k 5 dwts	100	175	225
locket with enameled portrait 14k 5 dwts	200	400	600
small religous cross plain14k 2 dwts	35	60	80
medium cross plain 14k 4 dwts	50	80	100
medium cross filigree 18k 4 dwts	75	125	175

GOLD PENDANTS WITH COLORED STONES

Listings in this category will refer to "medium" size stones which would be cabochon or faceted round stones 15 mm or less in diameter or rectangular shapes which measure approximately 10 x 15 mm. "Large" sizes would refer to rounds over 15mm in diameter and rectangle cuts larger than 10 x 15 mm. All listings will be for stones in simple gold frames or mounts- more ornate frames or the addition of small diamonds will add value.

amber drop medium size	40	75	100
amber drop large	75	150	175
amethyst medium	75	150	200
amethyst large	100	200	250
aquamarine medium	150	250	300
aquamarine large	200	400	500
citrine medium	100	175	225
citrine large	150	300	400
coral bead style	75	150	200
coral fancy carved	150	300	400
garnet medium	65	100	125
garnet large	100	175	225
jade medium bead or cab	150	300	400

jade carved medium	150	250	300
jade large carved	200	350	500
lapis lazuli medium	75	150	200
lapis lazuli large	100	200	250
moonstone medium	75	125	150
moonstone large	100	150	175
opal medium	75	150	200
opal large	150	250	325
pearl	refer to pearl section		
peridot medium	75	150	200
peridot large	100	200	300
topaz medium	100	175	225
topaz large	150	300	400
tourmaline medium	100	175	225
tourmaline large	125	250	350
turquoise medium	75	125	150
turquoise large	100	175	250

PENDANTS WITH SMALL DIAMONDS

This section will list the general values of filigree drops, crosses and other pendants which are set with small diamonds, the listings include gold or platinum mounts and matching light to medium weight chains. Pendants with large diamond solitares as the focal point as well as pendants with larger emeralds, rubies and sapphires should be appraised and evaluated on an individual basis due to the variety of sizes and quality levels of the gemstones.

diamonds tw .15-.20 ct	125	200	300
diamonds tw .25-.30 ct	200	300	350
diamonds tw .35-.45 ct	200	350	400
diamonds tw .50-.65 ct	300	450	500
diamonds tw .70-.80 ct	400	600	750
diamonds tw .85-1.00 ct	550	850	1000

PENDANTS

Emerald 12 ct cabochon,17x20mm platinum with diamonds (tw .60 ct), plat chain
c.1910
2500 3500 4000

Religous Mother of Pearl cameo, 23x41 mm filigree platinum frame, wg neck chain, sm diamond
c.1920
350 500 600

Mother of Pearl cameo religious, plat frame 23x46mm sm diamonds (tw.20 ct) plat chain c.1910
500 700 800

Enamel portrait pendant, 18k frame, 29mm polychrome enamel, with locket opening on back 25" 18k neck chain
c.1890
600 800 900 ✩✩

Amethyst and small pearl, Victorian 18k 16x50mm with gold chain c.1890
300 450 550

Enameled pendant full color, 18k frame, 25x39mm with three sm diamonds and gold neck chain, c.1910
350 550 650 ✩

PENDANTS

Gold with diamonds (tw .20 ct) and small square cut rubies, 18k, 25mm diameter with neck chain, c.1905
250 400 500

Filigree platinum sm diamond (tw .05 ct) 11x25 mm Victorian, with chain c.1885
150 300 400

Gold cross with six rose cut diamonds, (tw .30 ct) 18k filigree work, 37x53mm, 4 dwts Victorian c.1880
300 500 600 ☆

Art Deco spider web, 18k 18mm with sm diamond, blue enamel on spider c.1930
300 450 550 ☆

Art Nouveau 18k raised relief profile, 26mm with chain 13 dwt total c.1910
200 350 450

Diamond and sapphire, platinum 12x20 mm, .12 ct tw diamonds with plat chain, c.1915
300 450 550

PENDANTS

Diamond and sm emerald pendant, 36mm long, 15 diamonds tw .60 ct, platinum with 18k chain c.1920
400 650 750

Diamond and sapphire, Edwardian 11x20 mm, platinum with matching chain tw diamonds- .30 ct   c.1910
300 450 550

Aquamarine and diamond, 18k wg, 7ct aqua, sm diamonds (tw .05 ct) 10x27 mm, wg chain c.1940
350 550 650

Ruby and sapphire small insect pendant, 13x16 mm, with 18k chain three cabochon rubies, one sapphire c.1940
200 325 425

Platinum and diamond "lucky 13" drop, 17mm with sm diamonds (tw .05 ct) Platinum chain c.1920
150 300 400

Onyx 16x24mm with platinum bale and frame, sm diamonds (tw .19 ct) plat chain c.1900
225 450 500

PENDANTS

Art Nouveau 18k raised profile with sm ruby 25mm with chain c.1900
250 400 500

Diamond and platinum bell motif, 11x12 mm, with chain, tw diamonds .35 ct   c.1905
300 450 550

Coin style 22mm 22k gold Aztec calendar design, border of sm sapphires and diamonds with 18k chain, tw 7 dwt c.1930
350 500 575

Diamond and platinum 30mm Maltese cross, 26 diamonds (tw .40 ct) with plat chain, Edwardian c.1910
300 500 600

Cross, platinum and diamonds, 21x39 mm sm diamonds (tw .30 ct) with chain c.1910
250 400 500

Ruby an diamond overlay initial pendant, 18k, 27mm, round rubies, mine cut diamonds (tw .80 ct) c.1920
300 500 600

PENDANTS

Diamond filigree with sm rubies, platinum 17mm, cushion and rose cut diamonds (tw .45 ct) sm marquise rubies c.1920
300 500 600

Jade Budda pendant, 18k pagoda with amethyst. carved jade 26x37 mm
14 dwt c.1920
250 450 550

Gold Etruscian revival pendant, 18k 38mm, with opal, peridot, beryl and garnets, 17 dwt
c.1890
200 400 500

Jade pendant 18k chain and leaf frame, carved jade drop 16mm long
15 dwt c.1930
200 300 400

PENDANTS

Etruscian revival pendant
18k with turquoise, and
amethysts, 7x10 mm, fine
granulation designs c.1905
200 325 400 ☆

Gold and enamel drop, 18k
33mm, central .05 diamond
3 dwt   c.1920
150 200 250

Art Deco diamond and sap-
phiro pendant, round single
cut diamonds (tw .75 ct) sm
sapphires, platinum chain
c.1930
300 500 600 ☆

PENDANTS

Diamond filigree
round pendant,
13mm, platinum with
diamonds (tw .40 ct)
sm sapphires c.1910
275 450 525

Enamel and gold 18k, 25mm,
center diamond .05 ct, red
white and blue enamel, 5 dwt
c.1895
150 225 275

Art Nouveau 22mm
10k frame with raised
profile of young lady,
ruby stone accents
3 dwt   c.1915
175 250 300

Diamond drop,
dangle style with
sm diamonds (tw
.40 ct) platinum
frame and 18k
chain Belle
Epoque period
c.1905
200 375 475

Art Nouveau
raised relief por-
trait 21mm 18k ,
3 dwt c.1915
100 200 250

PENDANTS

Art Nouveau 18k 27mm
detailed profile of lady
3 dwt c.1915
150 275 325

Gold "griffin" motif
with diamonds (tw
.30 ct) sm rubies,
18k with chain
24mm c.1930
200 400 500

Ruby and diamond horse-
shoe "J" motif, 18k, 33mm
with chain, 17 dwt, tw diamonds .15ct c.1925
350 600 700

Gold cross with sm
diamonds and
rubies 18k, 22x42
mm 3 dwt
c.1900
150 300 400

Platinum diamond and
sapphire drop, 11x25
mm, with chain,
tw diamonds .30 ct
c.1915
300 450 550

PENDANTS

Gold initial pendant with
sapphires and diamonds
(tw .25 ct) 18k,5 dwt
11x65 mm, late Victorian
c.1895
300 500 600

Gold cross large Victorian style 18k,
47x74 mm fine granulation, small
pearl, 5 dwt, c.1870
200 350 450 ☆

Platinum cross 28x54mm
small pearls and diamonds
(tw .35 ct)
c.1910
250 400 500

Pearl and diamond
cross, platinum .15 ct
tw diamonds, 22x32
mm c.1895
175 300 400

PENDANTS

Small 18k cross,18x30mm small diamonds and half pearls c.1885
175 275 375

Religous pendant Joseph and infant Jesus motif 18k and platinum frame 31mm sm diamonds (tw .60 ct) and emeralds with gold chain 8.8 dwts c.1915
400 600 700

Victorian pearl and gold locket, onyx center, 18k with rose cut diamonds sm emerald at center, 24x28 mm c.1880
500 800 900 ☆☆

Art Nouveau 18k raised relief lady, 26mm 3dwt c.1915
150 225 275

Heart pendant with sm pearls, .25 ct cushion cut diamond, 18k frame and chain c. 1890
200 400 500

PENDANTS

Gold fob pendant
30x31mm, 18k , 11 dwts,
ornate with cabochon
coral, carnelian and
topaz, gold chain, c.1880
250 400 500

Jade and 18k pagoda
pendant, 28x32 mm, with
chain, 12 dwt c.1930
200 350 400

Coral Budda pendant
18k, 25x35 mm, with
chain, 11 dwt c.1950
250 400 500

Gold peacock with sm opal,
ruby, and sapphire accents,
14k, 35mm, 11 dwts, c.1950
250 400 500

Victorian turquoise, onyx, and
pearl locket 14k, 30x48 mm
black enamel line accents, 18
dwts c.1870
400 700 800 ☆☆

PENDANTS

Carved coral Budda pen-
dant, 18k horseshoe frame
with sm rubies,
29x38 mm, 14k chain
10dwts c.1950
175 350 450

Opal and diamond
pendant, 8x9 mm
cab opal, round dia-
monds (tw .80 ct)
18k chain, 4.3 dwts
c.1950
400 600 700

Ruby and diamond,
platinum mount, 7x8
mm cab ruby, thirty
rose cut diamonds, 14k
wg neck chain, Art
Deco c.1920
500 900 1100 ☆

Citrine pendant, 13x18x20
mm facetted citrine, 14k
mount with diamonds
(tw .80 ct) 14k chain 12dwts
c.1950
250 500 600

PINS AND BROOCHES

This section will present the many different styles of collectible antique pins and brooches. The photographs will be divided into the following sections.

Bar pins and filigree pins with small gemstones
Diamond brooches and pins with gem weight over 1.00 Ct
Floral, fancy form and sporting motif pins and brooches
Victorian memorial brooches,enamel and portrait pins
Colored gemstone brooches and pins

Note: Stickpin brooches will be listed in the stickpin section
Pearl pins are featured in the pearl section and cameo
brooches are found in the cameo section.

BAR PINS AND FILIGREE PINS WITH SMALL GEMSTONES
Pins and brooches in this category are valued based on design, condition, material (gold or platinum) and the number and quality of gems. The designation "plain" will refer to pins without gem stones yet the pin may have some engraved patterns. The pins will average about 10 mm x 50 mm in size.

plain rectangular bar 10k 5dwts	30	60	100
plain rectangular bar 14k 5 dwts	40	75	125
plain rectangular bar 18k 5 dwts	65	100	150
filigree plain 10k 5 dwts	40	75	110
filigree plain 14k 5 dwts	50	90	140
filigree plain 18k 5 dwts	70	125	175
filigree plain platinum 5 dwts	100	150	200
bar pin 18k 5 dwts .05 ct diamond	75	125	175
bar pin 18k 5 dwts three dia (tw .15 ct)	125	200	250
bar pin 18k 5 dwts three dia (tw .30 ct)	175	275	325
bar pin 18k sm sapphires sm dia (tw .40 ct)	200	350	450
filigree pin 18k 3 dwts sm dia (tw .45 ct)	175	300	400
filigree pin platinum 4 dwts sm dia (tw .55 ct)	225	400	500
filigree plat and dia (.60 ct center, tw .90 ct)	600	900	1200

DIAMOND BROOCHES AND PINS WITH
TOTAL WEIGHT OVER 1.00 CT

Brooches and pins in this category were very popular in the Edwardian and Belle Epoque periods of 1900-1920. Platinum was the new metal prefered by jewelers since it lent itself to fine filigree work and lace like designs which were now in vogue. Diamonds also came to the forefront during this period with the discovery of new mines and cutting techniques.

The listings in this section will represent items in 18k or platinum frames and mounts. The main stones will be mixed size diamonds of good color and clarity. Smaller emerald, ruby or sapphires will also be listed but sizes will be mentioned only on the larger more important stones. In evaluating brooches and pins of this style always look at the quality of the gemstones as well as the overall design. Frames and mounts should be in good condition. The quality of the setting is also important. Pieces which are roughly crafted or heavy in the metal work aspect are less desireable than finely crafted frames. Each line listing will begin with a total number of diamonds the piece would have. This number is given so the reader has an idea of the general size (weight) of the diamonds which make up the piece. The important number however is the total weight of the diamonds.This is the basis for the price structure.

20 diamonds tw 1.00 ct	400	700	900
20 diamonds tw 1.00 ct , sm rubies	500	800	1000
20 diamonds tw 1.00 ct , sm sapphires	500	800	1000
50 diamonds tw 1.50 ct	600	1000	1250
50 diamonds tw 1.50 ct , sm emeralds	750	1200	1500
50 diamonds tw 2.00 ct	850	1500	1900
75 diamonds tw 3.00 ct	1200	1800	2250
40 diamonds tw 3.00 ct	1500	2500	3000
50 diamonds tw 5.00 ct	2500	4000	5000
100 diamonds tw 6.00 ct	3000	5000	6000
150 diamonds tw 8.00 ct	4250	6000	7000
150 diamonds tw 10.00 ct	6000	9000	12000

FLORAL, FANCY FORM AND SPORTING MOTIF PINS

Pins in this category are often related to the Art Nouveau and Art Deco periods. Jewelry design was leaning towards naturalist forms with bird, flower, animal and sporting motifs. The pricing structure of these style pins must therefore relate to the artistic design as much as to the gems the piece is crafted from.

FLORAL, FANCY FORM AND SPORTING MOTIF PINS

flower pin 25 mm, 14k, 5 dwts	75	125	175
flower pin 25 mm, 18k, 5 dwts	100	150	200
two tone flower pin, 18k, 5 dwts	125	200	250
flower pin large, 50 x 70 mm, 18k 10 dwts	175	300	400
animal pin, small, 35 mm long, 18k 3 dwts	100	175	225
animal pin, medium, 42 mm long, 18k 5 dwts	125	200	300
animal pin, large, 48 mm,18k, 10 dwts	150	300	400
sporting motif 18k, 3 dwts, 10 dia tw .15 ct	150	225	300
sporting motif 18k, 3 dwts, 10 dia tw .25 ct	200	300	400
sporting motif 18k sm rubies, diamonds (tw .25 ct)	250	375	450

VICTORIAN MEMORIAL BROOCHES
ENAMEL AND PORTRAIT PINS

Victorian mourning or memorial jewelry became very popular in England after the death of Prince Albert in 1861. This genre usually features large brooches which had a locket area to hold a loved ones' lock of hair. The frames were usually ornate and set with popular Victorian motifs such as garlands, bows, arrows, hearts, crosses etc. Brooches from this period are highly collectible. Enamels, painted ivory pins and reverse glass paintings are also represented in this section. Generalized prices for these items can only be given on a broad "ball-park" basis since the quality, design and workmanship can vary greatly from piece to piece. Estimated prices will follow and all photo examples will be listed with more specific prices.

Victorian small 18k	125	200	300
Victorian medium 18k	175	300	400
Victorian large 18k	300	450	500
Victorian large with stones 18k	350	500	600
Victorian with enamel 18k	350	500	600
Victorian automated 18k	550	800	1000
enameled flower small 18k	200	350	450
enameled flower medium 18k	300	500	600
enameled portrait small 18k	200	400	600
enameled portrait medium 18k	300	500	700
painting on ivory small 18k	200	350	450
painting on ivory medium 18k	300	450	550
painting on ivory large 18k	400	550	700

COLORED GEMSTONE BROOCHES AND PINS

Jewelry examples in this category can vary greatly as far as the size, number, and quality of the stones. In evaluating colored gem brooches the value will be based on a combination of the main gemstone(s) value, the secondary (small diamonds etc.) gem value, and the value of the frame or setting. The workmanship, design and condition also factors which relate to the value.

133

BAR PINS AND FILIGREE PINS

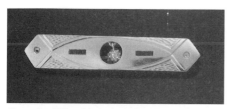

Bar pin 18k with sm rubies 55mm,
central diamond dangle (tw .05 ct)
 c. 1910   100 150 200

Bar pin 18k with small half pearls, 60mm, white
enamel edges 4 dwts c.1905
200 300 400

Bar pin 18k rose cut diamonds (tw .15 ct)
11x49mm 3 dwts c.1890   125 175 225

Bar pin 18k sm rubies, six sm rose
cut diamonds 12x50mm 3 dwts
c.1905   175 275 325

BAR PINS AND FILIGREE PINS

Bar pin with diamond (.08 ct)
18k, 11x46 mm with ruby line
accents, 3 dwts c.1910
175 275 325

Diamond bar pin 18k 10x45 mm with
three diamonds (tw .30 ct) 3 dwts
c.1905
175 225 300

Pearl and diamond bar pin, 18k
small diamonds (tw .30 ct) five
pearls 40 mm long, Victorian
c.1890
200 300 400

Victorian bar pin, half pearls and
sm center sapphire, 18k 56mm
long 4.2 dwts
c.1890
250 325 400

Bar pin with flower motif
and sm diamond, 18k rose
and green gold 51mm 2.5
dwt c.1900
175 250 300

BAR PINS AND FILIGREE PINS

Art Deco bar pin 18k, circle of sm rubies, sm side diamonds,
80 mm long c.1930
350 450 500

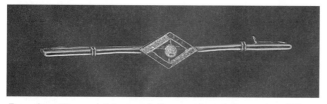

Bar pin with sm rubies and diamonds, platinum top 18k
back, 65 mm long c. 1920   200 300 400

Diamond bar pin with two sapphires, 70mm
long, platinum on 18k, tw diamonds approx
.40 ct c.1910   275 375 450

Bar pin, center sapphire
4.5x6.5 mm, sm diamonds
(tw .30 ct) 75 mm long,
platinum on 18k 3.5 dwts
c.1910
300 400 500

Diamond and sapphire pin, platinum on 18k, five diamonds
(tw .25 ct) four sapphires, 84 mm long 3.2 dwts c.1905
350 450 550

BAR PINS AND FILIGREE PINS

Linear style pin, platinum on 18k 48mm long, three cushion cut diamonds (tw .40 ct) c.1920
225 300 400

Bar pin center diamond (.05 ct) two sm sapphires, platinum on 18k 45mm. 1.5 dwt c.1920   100 150 200

Bar pin with cabochon sapphire (3.5x4.5 mm) ten sm diamonds (tw .20ct) 48mm long c.1910
200 300 400

Gold bar pin 18k with sm square cut rubies, central circle motif with sm diamonds, 54mm 2.5 dwt c.1910
175 275 325

Bar pin 18k with channel set square rubies, .05 ct diamond 49mm long c.1920
200 300 400

BAR PINS AND FILIGREE PINS

Bar pin with sm rubies and diamonds (tw .30 ct)
62 mm long, 18k 3 dwts c.1920
200 300 400

Diamond filigree bar pin, sm diamonds (tw .55 ct) platinum on 18k, 81 mm long 4 dwt c.1895
300 400 500

Diamond filigree pin, platinum 77mm long, sm rose and cushion cut diamonds (tw .50 ct) 4 dwts c.1895
250 350 425

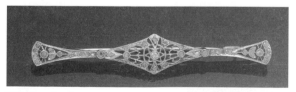

Filigree pin 18k wg with single cut diamonds (tw .45 ct)
67mm long 3 dwts c.1900
200 300 400

BAR PINS AND FILIGREE PINS

Victorian platinum pin, 11x65 mm ten sm diamonds
(tw .30 ct) three sapphires 5 dwts, c.1895
550 700 800

Pearl and diamond filigree pin 14k, 64 mm long,
central .08ct diamond seed pearls, 4 dwts, c.1900
175 250 325

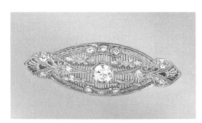

Filigree pin 16x42 mm, central .60 ct diamond. sm outer
diamonds, (tw .90 ct) platinum, Edwardian c.1900
700 900 1100

Victorian diamond and pearl
brooch, fifty diamonds (tw
2.05 ct), platinum mounts,
central pearl, 15x26 mm
c.1890
1200 1600 2000 ☆☆

DIAMOND BROOCHES AND PINS

Diamond and ruby flower brooch, 18k, 35x54 mm, 13 dwts. cabochon rubies, 123 diamonds (tw 6.30 ct) c.1920
3000 4500 5500 ☆☆

Diamond bow motif brooch, 23x50mm, 1.12 ct light canary center diamond, 48 outer diamonds (tw 2.5 ct) filigree platinum mounts c.1890   2000 3500 4250 ☆☆

Edwardian brooch, platinum with center sapphire (1.75 ct) 42x51mm total diamond weight 4.50 ct , 10 dwts c.1900
3000 5000 6000 ☆☆

Filigree diamond bar pin, 17x79 mm platinum with 39 diamonds (tw 1.60ct) sm triangular sapphires, 6 dwts c.1900   1200 2000 2500 ☆☆

DIAMOND BROOCHES AND PINS

Floral diamond spray pin, numerous diamond with tw 2.00 ct, (center stone is .70 ct) 18k wg, 6 dwts, 39x59 mm, Edwardian c.1910
1500 2500 3000 ☆ ·

Diamond and sapphire filigree pin, 14x88 mm, twenty sapphires, thirty five diamonds (tw 3.00 ct) platinum setting, late Victorian, c.1890 1800 2800 3500 ☆☆

Diamond and ruby brooch 52x62 mm, platinum with sm round rubies, numerous diamonds (tw 9.00 ct) 26 dwts, Victorian c.1880
5000 8500 10000 ☆☆☆

DIAMOND BROOCHES AND PINS

Moon and star motif brooch, round diamonds (tw 2.25 ct) in platinum over 18k frame, 32 mm c.1915
1200 1800 2400 ☆

Diamond and emerald brooch, 25x49 mm, forty-four diamonds (tw 8.25ct) 3.75 ct emerald at center, 12 dwts c.1890   6000 10000 12000 ☆☆☆

Diamond filigree pin, 17x70 mm, fifty five diamonds (tw 1.55 ct) platinum, 6.3 dwts c.1885   600 1000 1250 ☆

Filigree diamond pin, platinum 16x72 mm seventeen diamonds (tw 1.0 ct) 5.4 dwts Edwardian c.1910   400 700 1000

DIAMOND BROOCHES AND PINS

Diamond and ruby pin, sixteen square cut rubies, twenty diamonds (tw1.00 ct) 14k wg 30mm diameter, c.1920
500 900 1200

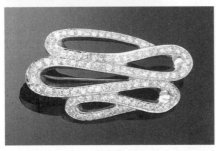

Diamond and platinum pin, ribbon design 24x44 mm, ninety-nine round diamonds (tw 3.00 ct) 9 dwts c.1920
1200 1800 2200 ☆

Diamond bar pin, 75 mm long, fifteen diamonds (tw 1.0 ct), platinum on 18k, c.1920
400 750 900

Diamond "leaf" pin, 23x47 mm, 18k wg with 2.7 ct tw diamonds, c.1915
1000 1500 1800 ☆

DIAMOND BROOCHES AND PINS

Diamond and platinum floral brooch, 52x72 mm, numerous diamonds total weight 7.00 ct, c.1930
3000 4500 5500 ☆☆☆

Diamond and platinum clips-brooch, converts from a 28x62 mm brooch to two clips, baguette and round diamonds (tw 6.60 ct) c.1920   3500 5500 6500 ☆☆☆

Diamond and sapphire circle pin, platinum, 45mm, 6 sapphires, 23 diamonds (tw 1.1 ct) c.1910
500 800 1000 ☆

DIAMOND BROOCHES AND PINS

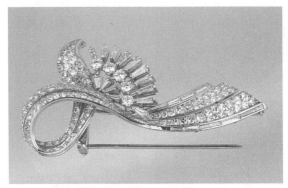

Diamond and platinum flower brooch, 63 mm
long, 14 dwts, 168 round and baguette cut diamonds (tw 7.75 ct) Edwardian c.1910
4000 5000 6500 ✩✩

Floral motif diamond brooch,
platinum, 45x30 mm, mix of
round, baguette and mar-
quise diamonds (tw 5.00 ct)
G/Vvs quality c.1910
2500 3500 4500 ✩

Victorian rooster brooch,
2-1/2" tall, 18k body set
with large baroque
pearl, 5.5 cts of rose cut
diamonds, synthetic
rubies, 17 dwts, c.1890
1800 2400 3000 ✩✩

FLORAL AND FANCY PINS

Large Art Nouveau flower brooch, 18k, 46x78 mm, central pearl, 12 dwts c.1910
350 450 550 ☆

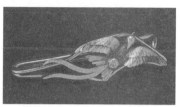

Art Nouveau bird pin, 18k wg and yellow, 14x47 mm, 5 dwts, sm diamond c.1915
250 350 450

Gold leopard pin, 18k, sm ruby eyes, 3.5 dwts, 41 mm, c.1930
300 400 500 ☆ ˙

Art Nouveau carnation flower brooch 18k, 50x73 mm, 9 dwts, central pearl c.1910
250 300 400 ☆

Floral brooch 18k with pearls, 70 mm long, 9 dwts, c.1915
275 375 475

FLORAL AND FANCY PINS

Rose and green
gold brooch, 18k,
54mm, 7 dwts
finely detailed
vine and leaf
motif, c.1920
150 250 350

Gold and sm pearl flower
pin 14k, 26 mm, 4 dwts,
sm central diamond
c.1920   150 225 300

Gold and gemstone flower
basket brooch, 34x42 mm,
18k, 12 dwts sm rubies,
sapphires, emeralds, pearl,
and diamond (tw .35 ct)
c.1930   600 950 1100 ☆ˌ

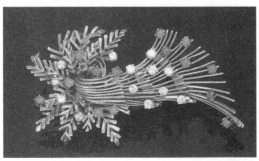

Gold floral spray
brooch, 18k with sm
turquoise and dia-
monds, 61 mm
long, 13 dwts, c.1940
450 600 750 ☆

FLORAL AND FANCY PINS

Etruscian Revival brooch, 18k dome style with fine granulation, sm rubies, 6 dwts, 32mm, c.1900
250 350 450

Gold dog motif bar pin, 18k, 39 mm, sm diamond 2 dwts, c.1930 250 350 450 ☆

Filigree pin with onyx and sm diamond, 20x23 mm, platinum on 18k sm seed pearls, 2.2 dwts, c.1890
225 375 475

Art Nouveau flower pin, 14k, 21x28 mm, sm pearl, 2.2 dwts, c.1910
125 200 300

Gold horseshoe pin, 18k, 23x27 mm, sapphires and diamonds (tw.20 ct) 2.3 dwts, c.1940
150 225 300

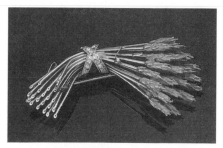

Gold and diamond pin, French 18k, superior details, sm diamonds (tw .15 ct) 56 mm long, 11 dwts, 22 fine "wheat stalk" pieces, c.1920   550 750 950 ☆

FLORAL AND FANCY PINS

Gold pin with moss
agate center, 35x38
mm, 18k, 6 dwts,
Victorian c.1885
150 225 300

Tiffany rock crystal
and 18k, 2" across,
set with sm dia-
monds, c.1915
700 900 1100 ☆☆

Gold and diamond triple flower bloom brooch, 18k with tw .20 ct
diamonds, 3-1/2" long, c.1930   800 1100 1300 ☆

SPORTING MOTIF PINS

Horseshoe pin, 18k, central
ruby, sm diamonds (tw .25 ct),
42 mm, 2 dwts c.1920
200 300 400 ☆

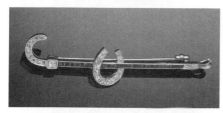

Ruby and diamond riding crop and
horseshoe, 18k, 52mm, channel set
square rubies, sm diamonds (tw .25
ct), 2 dwts c.1920
300 400 500 ☆

Sapphire and diamond riding
crop pin, 18k, 50 mm, sm diamonds, channel-set sapphires,
1.5 dwt, c.1920
200 325 425 ☆

Riding crop pin, 18k with sm
rubies and .20 ct tw sm diamonds, 54 mm double
horseshoe at center, c.1920
250 350 450 ☆

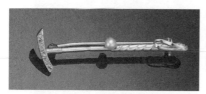

Gold and diamond "polo mallet"
pin, 18k, 46mm, 2.3 dwts, eight
small rose cut diamonds, round
pearl, c.1920
175 250 325 ☆

Jockey and dog motif, 18k with
enamel on jockey's cap, 55mm
long 3 dwts, c.1920
300 450 500 ☆☆

VICTORIAN AND MEMORIAL PINS

Victorian photo brooch, 18k, 48x75 mm, half pearl and black enamel accents, 10 dwts, c.1875
350 500 600 ☆

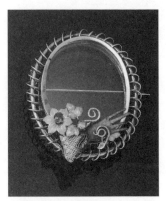

Brooch with photo/ memorial frame, 14k, 42x50 mm, sm pearl and ruby accents, white enamel flower basket, 11 dwt, c.1880
500 700 800 ☆

Gold and coral bird brooch, 38x42 mm, 18k, 8 dwts, c.1875
300 500 600 ☆

Victorian brooch, black enamel, pearls and sm turquoise, 39x52 mm, 18k, 8 dwts, c.1880
250 400 500 ☆

VICTORIAN AND MEMORIAL PINS

Enamel buckle motif pin, 18k sm half pearls, black enamel, 30 mm 4.5 dwt c.1890
250 400 500

Gold and pearl brooch, 18k, 3 dwts, 20x34 mm, small pearls, c.1890
150 225 300

Gold brooch with amethyst, 14k, 37x40 mm, 4.5 dwts c.1880
350 450 550 ☆

Victorian brooch, 18k with black enamel accents, 40 mm, sm rose cut diamond, c.1885
350 450 550 ☆

VICTORIAN AND MEMORIAL PINS

Victorian photo
brooch, 44x70
mm, 10 dwts,
14k, c.1875
250 375 450 ☆

Gold memorial locket,
38x44 mm, 14k, 5.5 dwts
leaf style frame c.1880
125 200 275

Large Victorian flower
brooch, 48mm, 18k
with six rose cut dia-
monds 6.5 dwts,
c.1875
400 600 700 ☆

VICTORIAN AND MEMORIAL PINS

Victorian brooch,
14k, reversible
center glass
frame, 46 mm,
10 dwts, sm
pearls and gar-
nets, c.1890
350 550 650 ☆

Gold memorial brooch,
14k, hair forms flower
motif set against Mother-
of-Pearl, glass front
45x50 mm, c.1870
300 450 550 ☆

ENAMEL AND PORTRAIT BROOCHES

Memorial pin with onyx and flower cameos, white carved flowers, fine 18k frame, revese side has locket with hair, 40x30 mm, c.1860
350 500 600 ☆

Exceptional painted ivory brooch, 18k frame, 31x38 mm, 6.2 dwts finely detailed and colored, c.1910
500 750 900 ☆☆

Rare enamel, diamond and emerald eagle brooch, 62x70 mm, 18k eagle is set with 148 diamonds (tw 2.5 ct), white and black enameled feathers, uncut 40 carat natural emerald base, 38 dwts, c.1930
1500 2500 3000 ☆☆☆

Victorian painted ivory brooch with diamonds (tw 1.00 ct), 27mm18k wg frame, 5 dwts, c.1880
900 1200 1500 ☆☆

ENAMEL AND PORTRAIT BROOCHES

Enamel and colored stone peacock brooch, 18k, 41x45 mm, multicolor enameled body, 10.5 dwts, opal, garnet, sapphire, amethyst accents, c.1930
400 600 850 ✫

Enameled dragonfly pin, 18k, 46x54 mm, 8 mm pearl, cloisonne enameled wings, 4.3 dwts, c.1920
200 350 500 ✫

Victorian enamel, pearl, and ruby brooch, 18k, 32x39 mm, blue, green and red floral enamel at center, outer pearls and sm rubies, 8 dwts, c.1875
400 600 700 ✫

Enameled pansy pin, 14k, 30mm, 5.5 dwts, blue, white and yellow shades of painted enamel, c.1920
350 450 550 ✫

Art Nouveau enameled
pin, 33mm, 18k, sm
pearls, green enameled
leaves, purple flowers,
c.1910
200 300 400

Limoge enamel and diamond
brooch, 14k, 20 round diamonds
(tw 4.00 ct), 2-1/8" across, full
color portrait with blues, gold, grey
and red hues, French
c.1940
1000 1850 2000 ✫✫

Enameled pin, blue,
grey and white portrait,
14k rose gold frame,
30x35 mm, c.1870
250 350 450 ✫

Reverse painting, 18k frame
32x42 mm, colorful bird motif,
Mother-of- pearl back, c.1890
250 350 450 ✫

COLORED GEMSTONE PINS

Amethyst and pearl pin, 18k,
32x22 mm, leaf frame, 5
dwts, c.1900
200 350 400

Citrine brooch, 14k fancy filigree
work, 40x44 mm, nine oval citrines-
light to med yellow color, c.1900
200 300 400

Coral bar pin, 18k, 65 mm long, 12 mm
coral center stones, sm side diamonds, 6
dwts, c.1920   200 350 450

Coral and diamond
brooch, 40x35 mm, 18k,
15 dwts, eight cabochon
light pink corals, sm diamonds (tw .15 ct) c. 1930
400 650 750

COLORED GEMSTONE PINS

Unusual coral pin, 18k, 3" long, deep red coral "branch", four
diamonds (tw .25 ct) baroque pearl (14 mm) signed JK,
c.1930   550 900 1100 ☆☆

Coral flower brooch, 45 mm
diameter, 18k, large coral
rose bud, sm emerald and
diamonds (tw .25 ct) accent
stones, c.1930
500 800 1000 ☆

Garnet and gold brooch, 14k,
40x40 mm, large cross design,
8 dwts   c.1880
250 400 500

Sapphire flower brooch, 14k, 42 mm
diameter, 8 mm cabochon sapphire,
fourteen smaller sapphires, 10 dwts,
c.1930
500 800 1000 ☆

COLORED GEMSTONE PINS

Rare black opal and diamond pin, large carved flower shaped opal
with round and navette shaped opals, 18k setting with diamonds
(tw .45 ct) 12 dwts, 63 mm long, superior quality, c.1930
1500 2200 2500 ☆☆

Opal brooch, 14k, 30
mm, eight diamonds
(tw .48 ct), central
cabochon opal (12x15
mm) 5.5 dwts c.1940
350 550 650

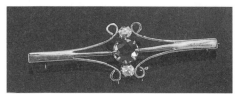

Sapphire and diamond bar pin, 1.2
ct sapphire, two .20 ct European cut
diamonds, 14k, 53 mm long, c.1920
300 450 550

Sapphire and diamond bar pin, 4 ct sapphire, fifteen
diamonds (tw 1.00ct) , 64 mm long, 18k, c.1910
600 900 1100 ☆

RINGS

Rings are easily the most popular form of jewelry and fine antique examples are always in demand. The majority of collectible rings date from 1880 to the Retro period of the 1940's and they will normally have gemstones as the main focal point. Plain "wedding band" types and gold signet rings are generally not collectible. This section will present rings in the following order:

Diamond solitare styles
Diamond "row" and eternity bands
Diamond clusters
Fancy, filigree and floral styles
Emerald, Ruby and Sapphire rings
Colored gemstone rings

DIAMOND SOLITARES Note: The cut, clarity, and color of diamonds always needs to be evaluated along with the carat weight. Since most solitare examples will be brilliant cut stones, this section will list prices for this type diamond in the J/Kcolor range and VS1-VS2 clarity. European cut and cushion cut diamonds will be valued at a lower rate than full brilliant cuts. All listings will be priced as in 18k gold mounts. Platinum settings are slightly higher in value.

solitare .25 ct	75	150	200
solitare .50 ct	250	500	750
solitare .75 ct	600	1200	1800
solitare 1.00 ct	2100	3750	5000
soiitare 1.50 ct	3500	6350	8450
solitare 1.75 ct	4100	7400	9850
solitare 2.00 ct	5400	9750	12950
solitare 2.50 ct	6750	12150	16200
solitare 3.00 ct	9750	17550	23400
solitare 3.50 ct	11375	20500	27300
solitare 4.00 ct	13800	24800	33100
solitare 4.50 ct	15500	27950	37250
solitare 5.00 ct	20500	37000	49000

DIAMOND ROW AND ETERNITY STYLE: The prices in this section will refer to diamonds of J/K color and VS1 clarity.

Five diamonds tw .40 ct 18k	125	200	250
Five diamonds tw .50 ct 18k	150	250	300
Five diamonds tw .60 ct 18k	175	300	325
Five diamonds tw .75 ct 18k	275	500	550
Five diamonds tw 1.00 ct 18k	400	700	750
Five diamonds tw 1.25 ct 18k	500	900	1200
eternity band platinum tw .30 ct	175	300	400
eternity band platinum tw .50 ct	225	500	700
eternity band platinum tw .75 ct	375	700	900
eternity band platinum tw 1.00 ct	550	1000	1200

DIAMOND CLUSTER RINGS

twenty diamonds tw .50 ct 18k	200	400	500
twenty diamonds tw .60 ct 18k	250	500	600
twenty diamonds tw .70 ct 18k	300	550	650
twenty diamonds tw .80 ct 18k	325	600	700
twenty diamonds tw .90 ct 18k	350	650	800
twenty diamonds tw 1.10 ct 18k	450	750	850
twenty diamonds tw 1.50 ct 18k	575	900	1100
twenty diamonds tw 2.00 ct 18k	900	1300	1500
forty diamonds tw 4.00 ct 18k	1500	2000	2500

DIAMOND RINGS-FANCY, FILIGREE, FLORAL: Rings in this category are priced by evaluating several factors. First, the total diamond weight is looked at along with the cut, clarity and color of the stones. Rings with a larger center or secondary stones will bring a higher value than rings which are made up of only smaller goods. Unless otherwise listed, the diamonds in this section will be European cuts. Brilliant cut stones will generally bring a higher value and cushion cuts will bring less. The use of small colored stones will also add value to rings especially when they add to the period look or design (Art Deco, Edwardian etc.) Finally, the overall condition and eye appeal of the setting should be considered. Fine filigree work and beatifully detailed floral designs will sell faster and for higher prices than roughly made or overly heavy types of mounts. The prices in this section will be listed in groups of three: the first entry will be for a ring composed of relatively equal size diamonds, the second listing will be for the same type ring (same diamond weight) but with the addition of small colored accent stones such as sapphires,emeralds, or rubies. The third entry will show the value of a ring with the total diamond weight being the same as the previous two entries but the ring will include at least one larger stone. For example, a tw .50 ct ring will be listed as .30 ct center, tw .50 ct.

This would represent a ring with a larger central diamond and then two or more smaller diamonds which make up the balance of the total. All examples will be listed as being in 18k mounts.

diamonds tw .30 ct	200	350	400
diamonds tw .30 ct + sm colored gems	250	400	500
diamond .20 ct center, tw .30 ct	275	575	650
diamonds tw .50 ct	300	525	625
diamonds tw .50 ct + sm colored gems	375	650	750
diamond .35 ct center, tw .50 ct	400	800	950
diamonds tw .75 ct	400	750	850
diamonds tw .75 ct + sm colored gems	475	950	1100
diamond .50 ct center, tw .75 ct	600	1150	1250
diamonds tw 1.00 ct	550	1000	1200
diamonds tw 1.00 ct + sm colored gems	700	1250	1400
diamond .75 ct center, tw 1.00 ct	875	1500	1800
diamonds tw 1.25 ct	625	1250	1500
diamonds tw 1.25 ct + sm colored gems	725	1500	1800
diamond 1.00 ct center, tw 1.25 ct	2000	3000	4000
diamonds tw 1.50 ct	750	1500	1800
diamonds tw 1.50 ct + sm colored gems	850	1800	2200
diamond 1.25 ct center, tw 1.50 ct	2500	3500	4500
diamonds tw 1.75 ct	875	1750	2100
diamonds tw 1.75 ct + sm colored gems	1000	2000	2200
diamond 1.50 ct center, tw 1.75 ct	3500	4500	5500
diamonds tw 2.00 ct	975	2000	2200
diamonds tw 2.00 ct + sm colored gems	1200	2500	3000
diamonds 1.75 ct center, tw 2.00 ct	4500	5500	6500
diamonds tw 2.50 ct	1200	2500	3000
diamonds tw 2.50 ct + sm colored gems	1400	3000	3500
diamond 2.00 ct center, tw 2.50 ct	6000	7500	8500

EMERALD, RUBY AND SAPPHIRE RINGS

Rings which have these precious stones as the main feature are difficult to categorize. The color, cut, size and clarity are all very important factors which relate to price levels. Since these are natural gemstones, the color and clarity will be different for each and every stone you see. The best way to enhance your understanding and appreciation for these gems is to view as many as possible and compare colors, clarity, and price levels. When making a purchase or investment in colored gems, it is also highly advisable to get not only one but two or more appraisals by trained and experienced gemologists. An overview of prices will follow along with numerous examples and detailed descriptions. By reviewing this information the reader should get a fairly good sense of how size and cut relates to value. The prices will always reflect the value for moderately colored stones which are in very good condition and free of any serious flaws or unattractive inclusions. All listings will bc 18k mounts with single emerald, sapphires or ruby stones. The addition of side diamonds or other secondary stones would increase the value. The size measurements are approximations given to show the average size to weight relationship of emeralds, rubies and sapphires. When judging the weight of emeralds, keep in mind that if an emerald were cut to the same size and proportions as a 1 carat diamond the emerald would weigh .80 ct. since the density of the stone is different. Also, a ruby or sapphire cut to the same size as a 1 carat diamond would actually weigh 1.15 ct. The abbreviation "cab" is used for cabochon cut stones and the listing "cut" will refer to faceted stones in this section.

emerald cab 3 ct	300	600	800
emerald cab 5 ct	750	1500	1700
emerald cab 10ct	1500	2500	3000
emerald cab 20 ct	3000	5000	7000
emerald cut .50 ct	200	400	550
emerald cut 1 ct	250	500	750
emerald cut 1.5 ct	375	750	950
emerald cut 2 ct	400	800	1100
emerald cut 3 ct	500	1000	1400
emerald cut 4 ct	800	1500	2000
emerald cut 5 ct	1200	2000	2500
emerald cut 10 ct	2500	4500	6000
emerald cut 20 ct	5000	9000	12000
ruby cab 1 ct	150	300	400
ruby cab 2 ct	250	500	600
ruby cab 3 ct	400	900	1100
ruby cab 5 ct	600	1200	1400
ruby cut .50 ct	200	400	600
ruby cut 1 ct	450	800	1000
ruby cut 1.5 ct	600	1200	1500

ruby cut 2 ct and larger	rare	rare	rare
sapphire cab 1 ct	150	250	350
sapphire cab 3 ct	200	400	600
sapphire cab 5 ct	350	600	800
sapphire cab 10 ct	600	900	1300
sapphire cut 1 ct	250	450	600
sapphire cut 2 ct	350	600	900
sapphire cut 3.5 ct	800	1500	1850
sapphire cut 5 ct	1250	2500	3000

COLORED GEMSTONE RINGS

The values in this section are based on the color of the main stone in the ring as well as the size, quality of cut, and level of clarity that the stone carries. As suggested in the previous section, the reader is encouraged to view as many colored gemstone rings as possible with an eye for the richness and uniformity of color the stone shows. The following price chart will represent colored stones which are faceted round cuts having an overall diameter of 10 mm (coral, jade, lapis lazuli and opal listings will refer to cabochon stones measuring 8 x12 mm). These examples will all be priced as if in 18k gold mounts. The color that the prices represent will be for stones in a medium grade. It is important to remember that these examples are basic reference points to help show general values. Superior grade color gemstones will bring much higher values than stones of the same size that are not as intense in color. After reviewing the basic price chart, the reader should look to the photo examples to see how variations in size and styles of settings can affect the value.

amethyst	75	150	200
aquamarine	200	350	500
cats eye	rare	rare	rare
citrine	150	300	400
coral	100	175	200
garnet	80	120	165
jade	250	500	650
lapis lazuli	100	175	200
opal	175	250	400
peridot	150	250	400
topaz	150	250	300
tourmaline	150	250	300
turquoise	50	125	150

DIAMOND SOLITAIRE AND ETERNITY

Solitaire, .95 ct
European cut,
18k rose mount
c.1920
650 800 1000

Solitaire, .75 ct
cushion cut, 18k
two tone mount,
c.1900
400 500 600

Solitaire, .90 ct
European cut, 18k
c.1915
650 950 1200

Diamond (.80 ct
European cut
round) two syn-
thetic side sap-
phires 18k wg
c.1920
700 900 1100

European cut dia-
mond 1.25 ct, with
small side diamonds
(tw 1.55 ct)
platinum c.1910
1850 2300 2750 ☆

Edwardian ring,
platinum filigree
mount, .90 ct euro-
pean cut round
diamond, c.1900
700 1000 1300

Platinum eternity
band, 24 round
diamonds (tw .72
ct), 2.5 mm wide
band c.1910
400 600 800

Platinum eternity
band, 30 round dia-
monds (tw 1.20 ct)
c.1905
600 1000 1400

Eternity band, 16
diamonds (tw .40 ct)
platinum, 2.5mm
wide, c.1920
250 375 500

DIAMOND ROW RINGS

Platinum eternity band, 12 round diamonds (tw .36 ct) 5 mm wide with pierced line patterns, c.1905
250 400 500

Three diamonds, tw .65 ct, Vvs quality, 18k wg, 8 dwts, c.1920
300 500 600

Three diamonds, European cuts, tw 1.40 ct, 18k, 5 dwts, c.1910
350 600 700

Three diamonds, tw .70 ct. European cut , 18k, 4 dwts, c.1915
300 450 550

Three diamonds, tw .90 ct, European cut, 18k, 3.5 dwts, c.1900
400 600 700

Three diamonds, center stone is .50 ct, two outer .30 ct, tw 1.10 ct, 18k rose, 6 dwts, c.1910
600 850 1000

Three diamonds, tw .80 ct, 18k, 3 dwts, European cuts, c.1920
300 500 600

Three diamonds, tw .65 ct, 18k yellow and wg, fancy engraved top and sides, c.1910
300 500 600

Three diamonds, center is .80 ct, two outer at .60 ct each, platinum, 3.5 dwts, european cuts, tw 2.00 ct, c.1920
1500 2500 3000 ☆

Five diamonds, 18k, 1.25 ct tw c.1920
500 750 900

DIAMOND ROW RINGS

Five diamonds, platinum, Vvs 1.00 ct tw, c.1910
375 600 750

Five diamonds, tw 1.00 ct, Vs quality, 18k wg c.1930
500 800 1000

Five diamonds, tw .60 ct, Vvs quality, 18k wg c.1940
250 400 500

Five diamonds, tw .75 ct, Vvs, 18k wg, c.1920
325 550 650

Five diamonds, platinum, 1.20 ct tw, c.1930
450 750 900

Five diamonds, 18k wg, .63 ct tw, Vs quality, c.1940
300 475 575

Five diamonds, 1.05 ct tw, Vvs, 18k wg, c.1930
400 700 800

Five diamonds, .95 ct tw, 18k wg, c.1920
350 600 700

Five diamonds, .44 ct tw, light canary color, 18k wg, c.1920
250 450 550

Five diamonds, cushion cut, .45 ct tw, 18k fancy Victorian mount c.1895
250 400 500

Five diamonds, .70 ct tw, platinum, Vvs clarity, c.1920
350 600 700

Seven diamonds, .42 ct tw, platinum, Vvs clarity, c.1920
250 400 500

DIAMOND CLUSTER RINGS

Swirl motif cluster, 29 diamonds, tw .70 ct, 18k fancy shank, wg mounts c.1930
400 600 700

Horseshoe cluster, 25 diamonds, tw 1.70 ct, 14k wg, 7 dwts, c.1940
600 800 1000

Victorian cluster, 22 diamonds, tw .60 ct, cushion cuts, 13mm wide top 18k with diamonds set in platinum, c.1895
300 500 600

Pave cluster, 52 diamonds, tw .80 ct, 14k wg plain band, 10 dwts, c.1940
300 500 600

Diamond cluster, 21 diamonds, tw 1.10 ct, 18k engraved shank, c.1930
350 550 650

Checkerboard cluster, 16 European cuts, tw 1.28 ct, 18k, 12 dwts, 17x18.5 mm top, c.1930
450 750 850

Pave diamond cluster, 15 cushion cut, tw .70 ct, 18k wg, 11.5 mm top, c.1915
300 500 600

Large cluster, tw 5.50 ct, 72 diamonds are pave set, 72 are brilliant cut and prong set, 15 dwts, c.1930
2000 3500 4000 ☆

Early cluster, 9 diamonds, tw .85 ct, heavy 18k mount with deep engravings, 16 dwts, c.1910
400 650 800

DIAMOND CLUSTER RINGS

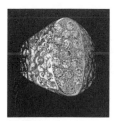

Pave style cluster, 19 diamonds, tw .95 ct, 18k, 8 dwts, textured shank, c.1950
375 600 750

Fancy cluster, 19 diamonds, tw 1.10 ct, 18k mount with leaf engravings 8 dwts, c.1920
450 750 850

Checkerboard cluster, 16 diamonds, tw .80 ct, 18k yg sides, wg top, 10 dwts, c.1930
350 600 700

Cluster 20 diamonds, tw 2.20 ct, 18k rope and flower petal design, 12 dwts, c.1940
800 1300 1500

Early cluster, 27 diamonds, tw 1.70 ct, 18k engraved band, 15 dwts c.1905
600 950 1200

Cluster, 28 diamonds, european cuts, tw 1.60 ct, diamonds set in plat., 18k band, 22 dwts, c.1910
600 950 1200

Diamond and sapphire cluster, 17 diamonds (tw 1.15 ct), 16 round cut sapphires, 18k, 5 dwts, c. 1940
500 750 1000

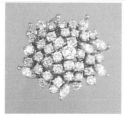

Floral cluster, 44 diamonds, round and marquise brilliants, tw 4.00 ct, platinum mount, c.1920
1200 2000 2500 ☆

FANCY FILIGREE FLORAL DIAMOND RINGS

Multi-diamond ring, 25 diamonds, tw 1.45 ct, 18k coiled design, 6 dwts c.1910
600 800 1000

Deco style, 16 diamonds, tw .30 ct, three row design with emerald stripe accents, 18k, c.1930
350 500 600

Horseshoe motif, 9 cushion cuts, tw .70 ct, 18k, c.1930
325 550 650

Victorian, three European cuts at center, sm single cut outer diamonds tw .28 ct, 18k, c.1895
150 225 300

Initial style, "S" with 14 diamonds, tw .55 ct, 18k c.1900
225 450 550

Question mark motif, 16 diamonds, tw .75 ct, 18k, european cut c.1900
350 600 700

Navette style, 15 diamonds, tw .80 ct, 18k, cushion cut c.1910
300 450 550

Floral design, five round and fifteen sm rose cut diamonds, tw .48 ct, 18k with platinum top, c.1890
250 400 500

Victorian, 17 cushion cut diamonds, tw .90 ct, center stone .45 ct, 18k c.1890
300 550 650

FANCY FILIGREE FLORAL DIAMOND RINGS

Swirl design, 17 diamonds, tw .50 ct, 18k wg, c.1930
200 400 500

Early Victorian, central rose cut weighing 1.25 ct, nine outer rose cuts, tw 2.15 ct, 18k original mount, c.1870
900 1500 1800 ☆

Edwardian 12 diamonds, tw .26 ct, platinum top with sm sapphires 10x 14 mm, 18k shank, c.1905
250 350 450

Diamond and sm rubies, five diamonds, tw .40 ct, 18k wg, c.1900
300 500 600

Diamond and emerald, 12 rose and European cuts, tw .40 ct, triangular emeralds, 18k and platinum, Edwardian, c.1900
325 550 650

Navette style, 15 rose cut diamonds, tw .80 ct, 18k setting, 11x21 mm Victorian, c.1880
300 500 600

Two diamond, European cuts, tw .75 ct, 18k wg, c.1910
275 450 550

Cross over design, 14 diamonds, tw 1.15 ct, 18k wg, c.1920
350 600 700

Cresent swirl, European center diamond .80 ct, 28 outer diamonds, pave set, tw 1.80 ct, 14k wg, c.1930
1000 1800 2000

FANCY FILIGREE FLORAL DIAMOND RINGS

Sapphire and diamonds, sm diamonds tw .35 ct, triangular sapphires, 18k and platinum, Edwardian c.1905
300 400 500

Filigree diamond and sapphire, European cut, tw 1.40 ct, platinum mount, 14x27 mm, sm rect sapphires, c.1900
700 1000 1300

Tremblant flower with diamonds, tw .77 ct, 18k with hinged petals and tremblant (spring style) center mounts, 11 dwts, c.1950
600 900 1100 ☆

Diamond ring, center European cut 1.04 ct, six outer diamonds, tw 1.28 ct 18k wg mount, c.1910
1500 2500 3000 ☆

Multi diamond ring, three center stones (largest is .25 ct), 16 outer diamonds, tw 2.25 ct, platinum and 18k mount, c.1895
800 1300 1500 ☆

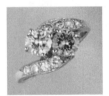

Cross over design, one 1.00 ct white diamond, one 1.00 ct treated blue diamond, 10 sm outer stones, tw 2.50 ct, 18k wg, c.1935
1500 2500 3000 ☆

Victorian clover motif, three diamonds, tw 1.09 ct, 18k rose, c.1890
300 500 600

Diamond navette, three center diamonds-.70, .90, .70 ct, 11 diamonds with tw 2.80 ct, platinum, c.1910
1800 2750 3270 ☆

FANCY FILIGREE FLORAL DIAMOND RINGS

Filigree with large diamond, center European cut 1.60 ct, sm outer diamonds, tw 1.90 ct, platinum, c.1910
2000 3000 3500 ☆

Diamond ring, center 2.45 ct European cut round Vvs/M, 12 outer diamonds, tw 3.45 ct, 18k fancy Victorian mount, c.1895
3750 5750 7000 ☆☆

Victorian flower ring, .20 ct center, 9 diamonds tw 1.30 ct, 18k mount, c.1890
500 800 1000

Navette diamonds (tw 1.5 ct), central emerald, 30 mm long, 18k Victorian c.1880
700 1200 1500 ☆

Diamond " ballerina " style, central 2.5 ct marquise emerald, 14k wg 32 baguette diamonds, 16 round brilliants, tw 4.00 ct, c. 1950
2000 3500 4000

Diamond ballerina ring, central 1.2 ct sapphire, numerous baguette and round diamonds (tw 2.00 ct), 14k c. 1950
700 1000 1500

EMERALD RINGS

Emerald 3.8 ct
round cab, 14k,
.05 ct diamond,
c.1940
400 500 600

Emerald 3.3 ct
cab, 18k with .28
ct tw diamonds, 6
dwts, c.1920
500 750 900

Double emerald ring,
two cabs (tw 2.75 ct),
18k with .26 ct tw dia-
monds
c. 1930
600 1000 1200

Muzo emerald, 3 ct cab, 14k with .40
ct tw diamonds, 3 dwts, c.1930
(emeralds from the Muzo mines are
prized for their fine color and trans-
parency--the clearness of the stone
allows the lower or interior levels to
show with fine clarity)
600 900 1200 ☆

Emerald cab, 5 ct , 18k
with diamonds (tw .65
ct) 16 dwts, c.1920
900 1500 1800

Emerald cab, 5 ct (10 x
12 mm) 18k, .24 ct tw
diamonds, c.1930
750 1250 1500

EMERALD RINGS

Emerald cab, 5.1 ct (10 x 12 mm), high quality with very good color, 18k with .55 ct tw diamonds, c.1920
1500 2200 2500 ☆☆

Emerald cab .75 ct (7x7.5mm) 14k wg with full cut diamonds (tw 2.00 ct), 5 dwts, c. 1920
2000 3000 3500 ☆

Emerald cab 4.5 ct (9x11 mm) with 20 diamonds (tw 1.20 ct), 18k wg 6.6 dwtc, c. 1920
1250 2000 2500

Emerald cab, 6.5 ct (17x21mm) 18k , sm diamonds (tw .06 ct) 10 dwts,   c.1930
700 1200 1400

Emerald cab, 10 ct (12x 13.5 mm) 18k fancy mount with 4 diamonds (tw .12 ct) c. 1920
1000 1700 2000

Emerald 15 ct cabochon (17x 13.5 x8.5 mm), 18k mount, 5 dwts c. 1900
750 1200 1500

Emerald cab with diamonds, "poison ring" -- emerald setting is hinged and opens to reveal a hidden recess, 19 ct emerald (23x28 mm), 18k wg mount with 20 diamonds (tw 1.50 cts) 9 dwts c. 1900
5000 6500 8000 ☆☆☆

EMERALD RINGS

Emerald step cut, 5x6mm, 18k with rose cut diamonds (tw .40 ct) c. 1900
300 450 550

Emeralds (two round .50 ct each) and one diamond (.50 ct cushion cut) 18k, 3 dwts, c.1910
500 700 900

Emeralds, three rectagular step cut, total emerald weight 2.5 ct, 14k with 16 diamonds (tw .65 ct) c. 1940
1200 1500 2000

Pear cut emerald 2 ct (11mmx 8 mm) 25 sm diamonds (tw 1.0 ct), 18k 10 dwts, c. 1920
700 1000 1200

Two pear shaped emeralds (5x10 mm) deep green, with diamonds (tw.36 ct) 14k wg, c. 1950
300 500 600

Step cut emerald 1.70 ct, 6.5 x 7 mm 14k wg with two .30 ct diamonds c.1940
600 900 1200

Emerald mixed cut 4 ct, 18k with 13 full cut diamonds (tw 2.60 ct), emerald has very fine color and clarity, c. 1920
2500 4000 5000 ☆☆

EMERALD RINGS

Emerald 4 ct step cut 10 x9 mm, 18k wg with 10 diamonds (tw .50 ct) c. 1930
800 1200 1500

Emerald 4.5 ct step cut 13x9.5 mm, 18k mount with 6 diamonds (tw .44 ct) c. 1920
800 1200 1500

Emerald 5 ct (15x13x8 mm), 18k with diamonds (.35 ct tw) 15 dwts very fine color and clarity, c.1920
1500 2500 3000 ✫✫

Emerald 5.4 ct, 18k plain mount, 5 dwts, c. 1950
800 1200 1500

Emerald step cut, 5.8 ct, heavy 18k mount with two .12 ct diamonds 11 dwts, c. 1930
900 1400 1700 ✫

Emerald 5.2 ct with 28 diamonds (tw .65 ct) 18k fancy setting, c.1940
1800 2800 3500 ✫

Emerald 5.5ct step cut , 14 diamonds (tw 1.85 ct), 18k wg, 5 dwts c. 1930
2500 3750 4500 ✫

Rare heart cut emerald 2 ct , with 48 diamonds (tw 1.0 ct), 18k, 3.5 dwts c. 1960
1500 2500 3000 ✫✫

Emerald 8.5 ct step cut , 11.8x13.3 mm, 18k two diamonds (tw .30 ct) 10 dwts, c.1930
1250 2000 2500 ✫

EMERALD RINGS

Emerald 12.25 ct, 18k
with .30 ct tw diamonds,
10 dwts, c.1930
2000 3000 3500 ☆

Emerald square step
cut 11.5 ct, platinum
with sm diamonds (tw
.72 ct) c. 1915
3500 6000 7500 ☆☆

Emerald 10 ct step cut with
very good color, 18k dia-
mond bezel (tw .45 ct), 14
dwts, c. 1930
3500 4500 5500 ☆☆

Emerald 8.8 ct step cut
with 4.0 ct tw brilliant cut
diamonds, 18k, 12.5
dwts, c.1935
4000 6000 7500 ☆☆

Emerald large step cut 20
ct, 27 diamonds, (tw 1.35
ct), 18k wg 9.7 dwts
c. 1940
6000 8000 10000 ☆☆☆

EMERALD RINGS

Gents large emerald ring, 12.5 ct ,
15mm mix cut, fine
rich color, 28 diamonds (tw 5.5 cts)
heavy and fancy
14k mount, c.1950
6000 9500 12000 ☆☆☆

Emerald, extra fine quality, square
mix cut 6.5 ct (10.5 x 10.5 mm)
platinum mount, two triangular diamonds (each weighs 1.25 ct)
5.5 dwts, c. 1930
8000 12000 15000 ☆☆☆

RUBY RINGS

Two rubies (tw .20 ct) and three dia-monds (tw .28 ct) , 18k c. 1920
175 250 300

Ruby cab, 1.25 ct, 18k wg filigree mount, c. 1910
200 300 400

Pear cut ruby, 1.5 ct, 14k wg c. 1940
200 350 425

Nine sm rubies and six diamonds (tw .25 ct), 14k rose 3.8 dwts. retro design, c. 1940
225 350 450

Two round cut rubies and two diamonds, (tw .40 ct), 14k wg c. 1930
250 400 500

Six round cut rubies and seven rose cut diamonds (tw .65 ct), 18k, 3 dwts c. 1925
300 500 600

Double ruby cabs, (tw 5 cts) with sm diamonds (tw .16 ct) platinum 6 dwts, c. 1920
325 550 650

Ruby and diamonds, 12 round cut rubies, 24 sm diamonds (tw 1.0 ct) 18k c. 1900
375 650 750

RUBY RINGS

Ruby cab 11 ct, (11x 13 mm), 18k with six diamonds (tw . 22 ct) 8 dwts c. 1930
600 700 800

Ruby ring 2 ct of round and oval mixed cuts, 12 rubies total, 14k, 7.5 dwts c. 1940
500 750 850

Ruby cab 12 ct, (10 x 13 mm), 18k with 10 diamonds (tw .36 ct) 11 dwts c. 1930
550 800 900

Ruby cab 9 ct (10 x12 mm), 18k fancy mount with diamonds (tw .40 ct) c.1920
600 1000 1200 ☆

Ruby cab 17x13 mm, 20 ct, (darker stone with purple undertones), 18k four diamonds (tw .20 ct), c. 1920
700 1100 1300 ☆

Ruby cab 3 ct (8 mm in diameter), 18k fancy mount with 12 diamonds (tw .48 ct) c. 1915
700 1100 1300 ☆

Ruby cab 15 cts, 18k with diamond bezel (tw .60 ct), 12 dwts, c.1920
800 1200 1400 ☆

Ruby cluster, 16 pear and marquise cut rubies, central .52 ct diamond, 10 sm baguette diamonds (total diamond weight is 1.25 ct), platinum c. 1915
800 1400 1600 ☆

RUBY RINGS

Ruby cab 17 ct with
outer diamond bezel (tw
.80 ct) 18k heavy and
fancy setting, 15 dwts,
c. 1930
850 1400 1600

Exceptional ruby cab,
19 ct, 18k fancy mount
with 24 diamonds (tw
1.44 ct) 17.3 dwts,
c. 1920
1800 3000 3500 ☆☆

SAPPHIRE RINGS

Sapphire cab, 6.5mm diameter, platinum with two sm tapered baguette diamonds, 3 dwt, c. 1920
200 300 400

Sapphire cab, 1.5 ct, 14k fancy setting with ladies profiles on each side, 3 dwts, Art Nouveau c.1920
200 300 400

Sapphire cab 5.4 ct, 14k wg with two .20 ct diamonds on the sides, 3 dwts c. 1930
350 550 650

Sapphire round cab 1.5 ct, with diamonds, 7 diamonds (tw .35 ct) platinum c. 1910
500 700 900

Sapphire 5 ct round cab, 18k, six diamonds, tw .24 ct. 18k, 6.6 dwts c.1930
500 700 900

Sapphire cab, 5.5 ct, 18k with 20 diamonds (tw .60 ct), fancy engraved shank, 10 dwt, c. 1920
500 700 900

Sapphire cab 12.7 ct, 18k with tw .50 ct diamonds, 10 dwts, c. 1920
600 900 1200

SAPPHIRE RINGS

Sapphire cab 15 ct, deep blue, 18k mount with 2 diamonds (tw .04 ct) 7 dwts c. 1940
500 700 900

Fancy sapphire ring, 2.5 ct cab, 18k setting with .25 cts tw diamonds set in a swirl motif on sides, 6 dwts, c. 1930
550 750 950

Sapphire 9.5 ct cab, 18k with sm diamonds tw .80 ct, c. 1915
550 850 1050

Sapphire 13.5 ct cab, 2 sm diamonds (tw .10 ct), 18k c. 1930
650 1100 1300

Sapphire 8.5 ct cab, 18k fancy setting with 16 diamonds (tw .42 ct) 17 dwts, c.1920
700 1100 1300

Sapphire 15 ct cab (19x8 mm) with fancy 18k mount, 20 diamonds (tw .60 ct) c.1910
850 1400 1700

Sapphire round cab, 8 mm diameter, 15 European cut diamonds (tw.80ct) 3 dwts, Victorian c. 1890
500 900 1100 ☆

Sapphire 3 ct cab, outer border of European cut diamonds (tw 1.20 ct) 18k 3 dwts c. 1900
800 1300 1600 ☆

SAPPHIRE RINGS

Victorian sapphire
ring, 3 ct (7x 10
mm), 14 cushion
cut diamonds (tw
1.20 ct) 18k
c. 1880
900 1500 1800 ☆

Sapphire cab 12
ct, in heavy 18k
mount set with
1.10 ct tw dia-
monds, 13 dwts,
rich and even color
c. 1950
1800 3000 3500 ☆ ☆

Rare lavender star
sapphire, 25 ct
(19x21mm) plat-
inum mount with
round and
baguette diamonds
(tw 1.20 ct), 9.5
dwts, c. 1015
2500 3500 4500 ☆ ☆

SAPPHIRE RINGS

Three sapphires
mix cut, tw 2.25
ct, 18k fancy
engraved mount,
3 dwts
c.1915
250 350 450

Single sapphire
1.5 ct, 7x10 mm,
14k, ribbed band,
6 dwts, c. 1950
250 350 450

Facetted sapphire,
8.5x11 mm, 18k 3.1
dwts, c. 1900
275 375 475

Central sapphire
4x10 mm, two
.20 ct side dia-
monds, 18k plain
mount, 4 dwts
c.1920
300 425 525

Rectangular
green sapphire
(5.5x7 mm), 1.10
ct, 18k with sm
side diamonds, 4
dwts, c.1930
300 500 600

Sapphire 1.05 ct,
oval cut, 14k plain
band, 8mm wide, 5
dwts c.1940
300 500 600

Retro period , sap-
phire (1 ct) with 10
diamonds (tw .65 ct)
18k, 10 dwts
c.1940
300 550 650

Green sapphire,
oval 2.4 ct, 18k
with sm side dia-
monds, 3.5 dwts
c. 1930
350 550 650

SAPPHIRE RINGS

Sapphire, cushion cut 4.5x6 mm, with .25 ct tw mine cut diamonds, platinum c. 1920
500 700 800

Sapphire and diamonds, central 2 ct sapphire, 10 sm triangular sapphires, 10 diamonds (tw .32 ct) platinum c.1910
700 1100 1300

Sapphire 5 ct, 18k with diamonds (tw .48 ct) c. 1920
900 1500 1800

Sapphire and diamonds, central 1 ct sapphire, 9 diamonds (tw 1.8 ct)
18k 4 dwts, c.1920
1000 1700 2000

Cornflower blue sapphire, 3.5 ct (8x 11 mm), with diamonds (tw 1.0 ct)
18k c. 1930
1200 1800 2200 ☆

Large sapphire, 18 carats (13x16 mm), 18 diamonds (tw 1.20 ct) 7 dwts.
18k, c. 1920
2000 3000 4000 ☆

Sapphire 5 cts with platinum mount and 77 diamonds (tw 2.50 ct), 6.5 dwts, c. 1950
3500 6000 7000 ☆ ☆

COLORED GEMSTONE RINGS

Amethyst 12 x 16 mm
step cut, 6 diamonds
(tw .12 ct),18k rose,
6 dwts, Retro c.1940
250 325 400

Amethyst 14.5 x 17 mm,
step cut, side diamonds
(tw .12 ct) and sm
square rubies, 18k, 8.5
dwts Retro, c.1940
300 400 500

Amethyst round
cut 14 mm diame-
ter, 10 diamonds
(tw .30 ct),
18k, 6 dwts,
c.1930
300 400 500

Amethyst, 18.5 x20.5
mm step cut, fancy
mount 18k, 14 dwts,
c.1940
350 500 600

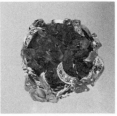

Aquamarine, natural
stones 18k with sm
diamonds, (tw .15 ct).
10 dwts c.1940
250 400 500

Aquamarine, 10x12 mm
oval cut , 14k, 5 dwts,
sm diamonds (tw .08 ct)
c.1950
300 400 500

Aquamarine, 8 ct step
rectangular cut, 13x10
mm, sm side rubies,
14k 6.5 dwts, Retro
c. 1940
400 550 650

COLORED GEMSTONE RINGS

Aquamarine, 8 ct square
step cut, 18k with dia-
monds (tw .60 ct) c.1940
400 650 750

Aquamarine 10 ct step
cut, 6 sm rubies, 8 dia-
monds (tw.32 ct), 18k
c.1930
400 650 750

Aquamarine 12 ct rectan-
gular, 2 diamonds (tw .14
ct), 18k 8 dwts c.1930
400 650 750

Aquamarine 11.5
mm round cut, sm
diamonds (tw .45
ct), platinum
5 dwts c. 1920
400 650 750

Aquamarine 12 ct
step cut, 18k with 6
diamonds (tw .18 ct)
10 dwts c. 1930
500 750 900

Aquamarine 12 ct
(13x16 mm) 4 sm
rubies, side diamonds
(tw .48 ct) 18k rose, 9
dwts, Retro c. 1940
600 800 1000

Aquamarine 12 ct
rectangular cut, sm
rubies, .60 ct tw of
diamonds, 18k, 8
dwts, c. 1940
600 800 1000

Aquamarine 12 ct
step rectagular cut,
18k with 2 dia-
monds (tw .12 ct)
8 dwts c. 1950
700 1000 1200

COLORED GEMSTONE RINGS

Aquamarine 11 ct
(18x11 mm) 6 diamonds
(tw .70 ct), 18k rose
mount c.1915
700 1100 1300

Aquamarine 20x15
mm (26 ct), step rec-
tangle cut, 14k wg
with 6 diamonds, (tw
.12 ct), c.1940
800 1200 1400

Aquamarine 20 ct
(14x15.5 mm), 14k
wg with 6 diamonds
(tw .30 ct) 5.5 dwts,
c. 1930
800 1300 1600

Aquamarine 30 cts
17x21 mm , cushion
cut, 14k with 10 dia-
monds (tw .80 ct), 9
dwts c.1950
900 1500 1800 ☆

Aquamarine 11x17
mm step rectangle
cut, very good
color, platinum
with numerous
pave set diamonds
(tw 1.20 ct) 8.3
dwts, c. 1920
1300 2200 2500 ☆

Aquamarine 35 cts, 23x23
mm, rich deep blue, 18k
wg mount with diamond
border (tw .65 ct), 13 dwts,
c.1930
1500 2500 3000 ☆☆

COLORED GEMSTONE RINGS

Cat's Eye 6.5x8 mm oval cabochon, good color, good "eye", platinum mount with baguette diamonds (tw .14 ct) 7 dwts c. 1920
1200 1500 1800 ☆

Cat's Eye 15.5x13 mm cabochon, rich greens, platinum mount with diamonds (.62 ct tw), 30 dwts, c.1920
3000 4500 5000 ☆☆

Cat's Eye 7.5x9.2 mm, very lively stone, strong "eye", first rate color, platinum, with sm side diamonds, 6.6 dwts, c.1920
3500 6500 7000 ☆☆☆

Citrine 16x22 mm step rectangular cut, 6 diamonds (tw .30 ct) 18k rose setting, 9 dwts, Retro c. 1935
250 350 450

Citrine 12x16 mm with sm rubies and diamonds (tw .18ct) 18k crossover design, 8.5 dwts, c. 1940
300 500 600

Coral oval cab (6x10 mm) with 12 rose cut diamonds (tw .25 ct), 18k 2 dwts, c.1920
250 350 450

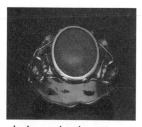

Jade oval cab (11.5x15 mm) 18k mount with dragon motif on sides 7 dwts c. 1920
300 400 500

Jade dragon ring, 14x15 mm cab, 14k dragon form mount, 8 dwts c.1930
400 600 700

COLORED GEMSTONE RINGS

Onyx (18x25 mm) set with a .15 ct round diamond, heavy 18k mount 15 dwts, c. 1950
250 400 500

Onyx (20x30 mm) set with 1 ct round emerald cab, platinum mount c. 1925
400 700 800

Opals, 2 ovals 3.3x4.2 mm with .25 ct oval diamond, 14k c.1920
150 225 300

Fire opal 10x14mm, 14k 3.3 dwts, c.1930
250 400 500

Opal 3 cts , fancy 18k mount, 10dwts, 6 diamonds (tw .25 ct), c.1930
300 500 600

Opal 5.3 ct (12x9 mm), fancy engraved 18k mount with 12 diamonds (tw .25 ct) 7 dwts, c.1920
375 650 750

Black opal, 2.1 ct (12.5x10 mm), 18k with 6 diamonds (tw.50 ct) 9.6 dwts c.1920
450 750 900

Opal and diamonds, eight 5x7 mm oval opal cabs, 10 diamonds (tw .50 ct) 18k, 10 dwts, c.1950
450 750 900

COLORED GEMSTONE RINGS

Opal 2.85 ct (18x10 mm)
18k fancy engraved
mount with 6 diamonds
(tw .40 ct) 10 dwts,
c. 1930
500 800 950

Black opal 5 ct (16x12 mm)
18k setting with 6 diamonds
(tw .50 ct)
c.1920
575 900 1050

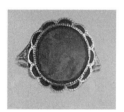

Black opal 11x12 mm,
intense colors, scal-
loped border with blue
enamel, 18k, 3 dwts
c. 1910
700 1200 1400 ☆

Black opal and dia-
monds, 10x44 mm
intense cabochon opal, 6
brilliant cut diamonds (tw
.80 ct) 14k wg 4.5 dwts
c. 1940
2000 3500 4000 ☆☆

Topaz 25 ct
square step cut,
18k with 8 dia-
monds (tw .16 ct)
9.5 dwts c.1940
275 450 550

Topaz 14x19 mm step cut,
18k with sm diamonds and 2
sm rubies 18k 8.8 dwts
Retro   c. 1940
275 450 550

STICKPINS

Stickpins are the true "miniatures" of the jewelers art. Animal and floral pins were very popular in the Victorian era. Cameo stickpins, diamond "question" mark pins and carved coral miniatures were also in vogue. The stickpins popularity continued during the Edwardian and Art Nouveau periods. The foremost Edwardian styles included lacy diamond pins, and pins with colorful combinations of diamonds with emeralds, rubies or sapphires. Stickpins from the Art Nouveau periods are quite scarce. The better examples of Art Nouveau portrait and enamel pins are very collectible. Art Deco period pieces are also highly desireable, yet difficult to find. Stickpins should be evaluated on a comparison basis. Look closely at the examples shown. Pay special attention to the detail and workmanship that the pin shows. That is the main value base. Also, note the gem weights given with the diamond stickpins since the values will relate in part to the total gem weight.

This section will be divided into the following types:

Animal form, fancy form and sporting motif pins
Diamond stickpins
Emerald, ruby, and sapphire stickpins
Enamel pins and unusual colored stone pins
Stickpin brooches (combination pieces with 3 or more pins)

ANIMAL FORM, FANCY AND SPORTING MOTIF

Native American
Indian motif, 14k,
14mm with sm ruby
in "pipe", sm
diamond c. 1910
200 400 500 ☆

Artists pallet, 18k,
8x12 mm, sm diamond and ruby
c.1915
75 125 175

195

ANIMAL FORM, FANCY AND SPORTING MOTIF

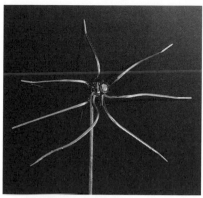

Spider pin, 45mm across, 18k with
sm diamond
c. 1900
75 150   200

Bird motif, 10x21 mm,
14k fine detail, sm
ruby eye, half pearls
Victorian c. 1890
75 150   200

Fox and diamond,
18k, 11x18 mm, .05
ct diamond, c. 1900
200 375 450

Diamond hum-
mingbird, plat-
inum top with sm
pave diamonds,
9x12 mm, ruby
eye, c.1920
175 350 450 ☆

Horse and diamond
horseshoe, 18k with
13 mine cut dia-
monds (tw .30 ct)
12x14 mm top,
c. 1910
100 200 350

Platinum horse with
diamonds, 11x12 mm,
sm rose cut diamonds
(tw .20 ct) 18k pin,
c.1905
200 400 500 ☆

Scroll design,
18k, 10x11mm,
with sm dia-
mond, emerald
and ruby
c.1910
100 200 275

ANIMAL FORM, FANCY AND SPORTING MOTIF

Rooster pin,
14x17mm, sm
rose cut dia-
monds, sm ruby,
18k with
platinum top
c. 1890
200 450 550

Lion pin with .20
ct diamond, 18k,
10x16 mm, 2.3
dwts c.1910
150 300 375

Snake and dia-
mond, 18k 9x12
mm, with seven
sm diamonds, sm
ruby eyes, sm
emerald on
snakes' head
c.1920
200 400 500

Fly stickpin, opal
body, ruby eyes,
seed pearls and
sm green stones,
14k, 12 mm long,
c.1900
200 400 500 ☆

Art Nouveau flower
pin, 18k, sm rose
cut diamonds, cen-
ter .10 ct diamond,
18 mm wide,
c.1905
125 250 300

Art Nouveau, lady in
profile, 14k, sm dia-
mond, 13 mm wide,
c.1915
125 250 300 ☆☆

DIAMOND STICKPINS

Circle pin, filigree,
10 mm, seven diamonds (tw .15 ct),
sm channel set
sapphires, 18k
c. 1910
125 250 300

Flower pin, 18k,
eight diamonds
(tw .40 ct) 15x12
mm,
c.1900
150 275 325

Crescent moon pin,
14k ,13 mm, seven
rose cut diamonds (tw
.30 ct) c.1895
125 250 300

Horseshoe, platinum
top with nine diamonds (tw .75 ct)
18k pin c. 1900
175 325 400

Floral pin, 12 mm
flower, 10 diamonds (tw .65 ct)
European cuts,
18k c. 1890
200 400 500

Leaf pin, 15 mine cut
diamonds (tw .30 ct),
18k and platinum,
11x17 mm
c.1900
125 250 300

DIAMOND STICKPINS

Circle pin, 12 mm diameter, central .30 ct diamond, sm outer diamonds (tw .45 ct) 18k and platinum c.1895
125 250 300

Ribbon bow design, 5 x17 mm, seven diamonds (tw .36 ct), platinum mounts, 18k pin c. 1895
125 250 300

Filigree pin, 14mm, thirteen diamonds (tw .10 ct) sm synthetic rubies platinum and18k, Edwardian c. 1910
125 250 300

Double horseshoe, 18k, 15x15 mm, sm rubies and round diamonds (tw .54 ct) c. 1915
200 400 450

Filigree pin, platinum top with sm rubies and diamonds (tw .40 ct) 18k pin, Edwardian c. 1905
175 350 400

Horseshoe 16x18mm, 18k with eighteen diamonds (tw .60 ct) c. 1910
350 400 450

Question mark motif, 10 x 17 mm, ten diamonds (tw .35 ct) 18k wg c. 1890
150 275 325

DIAMOND STICKPINS

Solitare diamond .70
ct diamond, 18k wg,
8 mm wide floral
mount
c. 1915
275 550 650

Diamond with onyx
accent stones, 9 x19
mm, platinum mount
with diamonds (tw
.66 ct) 14k pin,
c. 1890
300 600 700

Diamond circle
motif. filigree 12.5
mm diameter, sm
rose cut diamonds
(tw .45 ct) 18k wg
c. 1895
125 250 300

Horseshoe pin 14x16
mm, 18k with thirteen
diamonds (tw 1.00 ct)
one ruby, c.1910
350 650 750

EMERALD, RUBY, AND SAPPHIRE STICKPINS

Sapphire, 6.5 x
10 mm oval sap-
phire, prong set,
18k c. 1910
175 350 400

Sapphire and dia-
monds, 10.5x12.5
mm sapphire (1.0
ct) and eleven
mine cut dia-
monds (tw .55 ct)
18k c. 1895
225 450 550

Emerald pear cut
6x11mm (2.00 ct)
eleven diamonds
(tw .50 ct)18k pin,
c.1920
400 800 950 ☆

Ruby 3.5x6 mm
tear-drop fancy
cut, upper sm
diamonds and
rubies c.1920
125 250 300

Ruby and dia-
monds, 13x13
mm square with
calibre rubies,
sm diamonds
central pearl,
c. 1920
125 250 300

Diamond with synthetic
ruby (7 mm high dome
cab) 18k, ten round
European cut diamonds
(tw 1.00 ct)
400 800 1000 ☆☆

EMERALD, RUBY, AND SAPPHIRE STICKPINS

Sapphire 4x7.5
mm pear cut,
twelve diamonds
(tw .60 ct) 18k
c. 1900
150 300 400

Sapphire oval cut
(15x16 mm) nine
European cut
diamonds (tw .90
ct) 18k wg
c.1905
350 700 900 ☆

Edwardian pin
with 3m calibro
sapphires, syn-
thetic triangular
sapphires five
diamond (tw .20
ct) 14 mm across
18k c.1905
150 300 400

Emerald with eight
diamonds (tw .40
ct), square emerald,
18k mount
9x11 mm overall,
c.1905
150 300 400

ENAMEL AND UNUSUAL STICKPINS

Rare enameled portrait stickpin, 16 mm wide, superior enameling on 18k sm ruby, emerald and six sm diamonds, flowing gold hair strands, Art Nouveau c. 1920
500 850 1000 ☆☆☆

Egyptian revival pin, blue, green, red and yellow enameled pharoah, sm diamond accent, 18k, 9x11 mm, c.1925
225 450 550 ☆☆

Rare Victorian "Pekingese" pin, 14k rose gold with dog collar and buckle style frame, 24 mm across, painted ivory with fine detail, c.1890
300 700 900 ☆☆

Black opal stickpin, 8x14 mm black opal with superior colors, 14k, c.1920
250 500 600 ☆

Pearl "bunny" pin, 7x10 mm design with a natural pearl forming the rabbits body, ruby eyes, sm diamonds on the14k wg body c.1900
300 600 700 ☆☆

Triple enameled flower pin, 26 mm across, three sm diamonds, 18k c.1920
250 500 600 ☆

STICKPIN BROOCHES

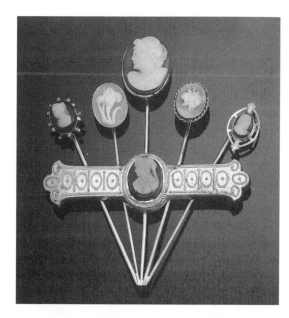

Multi cameo brooch, 60x70 mm with four stone cameos and two shell cameos, 14k pins, gilt center bar, c.1900
400 700 900 ☆☆

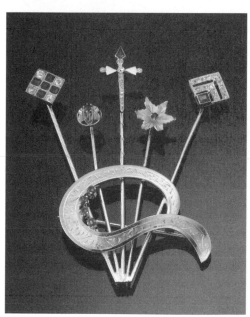

Diamond and ruby stickpin brooch, 18k, 56x71 mm, numerous rubies and diamonds (tw.30 ct) 10 dwts, c.1910
750 1500 1750 ☆☆

STICKPIN BROOCHES

Garnet stickpin brooch, 51x55 mm, five garnet
stickpins, 14k pins, central garnet and 10k
bar, Victorian c. 1885
300 600 700 ☆☆

Jade multi pin
brooch, 66x90 mm,
four jade cabochons,
14k flower pin with
sm round jade
stones, 11 dwts
c. 1930
300 600 700 ☆

STICKPIN BROOCHES

Turquoise brooch,
50x100 mm, 18k with
five turquoise pins,
sm diamond accents,
18 dwts, c.1930
500 1000 1200 ☆☆

Art Nouveau stickpin brooch, five pins with
amethyst, pearl and citrine centers, 18k, 63x83 mm,
13 dwts, c.1910
600 1200 1400 ☆☆

ASHLAND OFFERS WHOLESALE LOTS ! ! !

AJ 1 **DIAMOND RINGS**-- Ladies 18k white gold ring with five diamonds set in a straight line design. Circa 1930's. The round dazzling diamonds are well matched in size color and clarity. The total diamondweight is between .20 and .40 ct. The settings are fancy designs with fine accents between the prong set mounts.
One ring---$200.00   Two rings--$350.00   Five rings--$750.00

AJ 2 **PEARL NECKLACE AND BRACELET**-- This two piece lot features an 18" long necklace and a 7" bracelet. The round cultured pearls are approx. 4.5 mm in diameter and very nicely matched. Both pieces feature 14k clasps. Mint condition. Circa 1960's.
Both pieces--$175.00   **Two sets--- $299.00**
Necklace only--$125.00   **Two necklaces--$210.00**
Bracelet only--- $75.00   **Two bracelets--$115.00**

AJ 3 **DELUXE PEARL NECKLACE**-- An impressive 48 " long this popular strand of cultured pearls measures approx. 4.5 millimeters. Beautiful luster and color. Circa 1960's.
One piece--$275.00   Two pieces--$500.00   Three pieces--$675.00

AJ 4 **DIAMOND SOLITARE RINGS**-- This super wholesale lot features the best buy you can find in a lady's sparkling diamond solitare. The round diamonds are set in attractive 18k yellow or white gold mounts and the color and clarity of the stones is very nice. Circa 1930's
.10 ct diamond $125.00   **.20 ct diamond $175.00**
.30 ct diamond $200.00   **.40 ct diamond $300.00**

AJ 5 **COLLECTIBLE STICKPINS**---A super assortment of mint condition antique stickpins. All are set with colorful stones in solid 14 or 18k mounts. The pins are also gold. This lot is also terrific for resale.
Five pieces--- $375.00   **Ten pieces--- $650.00**

AJ 6 **DELUXE DIAMOND STICKPIN LOT**--- A limited time offer, this great lot gets you a wonderful, high quality diamond stickpin from the 1930's. Mint condition with a 14k or 18k gold mount and pin. You can order this item as a fancy diamond cluster style or as a larger diamond solitare style. Please indicate your preference when ordering.
One pin---$100.00   Two pins--$175.00   Three pins-- $225.00

AJ 7 **GRAB BAG LOT**--- This lot is a super assortment of colorful, distinctive, fine quality costume jewelry from the 1930's to the 1970's. Fun to coll- lect, the styles and "fashions" are eye catching and the lot features a mix of bracelets, rings, pins, necklaces etc. A super lot for yourself or use it for gifts or for resale.
Twenty pieces--$125.00   **Forty pieces-----$225.00**

AJ 8 **LADYS RETRO PERIOD GOLD BRACELET WATCH--** A fabulous look, this 18k gold bracelet watch is Swiss made, manual wind, circa 1930's. The stunning case and bracelet are solid gold and produced with bold curved and ribbed links from the Retro period. Professionally restored. Mint condition. The basic model is without gemstones and the premium model comes with small diamonds which ornament the top and bottom case areas.
Basic model-------$450.00 **Premium model--$650.00**

AJ 9 **LADYS HUNTER CASE POCKETWATCH--** In running condition, this fancy engraved watch was produced in the 1890- 1920 era and is highly collectible. Watches of this style were popular as pendants in the late Victorian times. The case features a closed cover over the superb white porcelain dial. A beautiful antique!
Gold filled case---$125.00 **14 k Gold case----$375.00**

AJ 10 **GENTS 1930-1940's RECTANGULAR WRISTWATCH--** Profoccionally restored, this 17 jewel wristwatch exhibits the clean distinctive styling of the Art deco and early retro periods. The timepiece is manual wind and very collectible. The gold filled case is near mint and the dial is superb.
One watch---- $95.00 **Set of five----- $395.00**

AJ 11 **LADYS ART DECO PERIOD WRISTWATCH----** Swiss made, circa 1930, this fantastic timepiece has the look of a high end platinum and diamond watch. The silver case is set with numerous rhinestones with a strong Art Deco styling. Fully restored. The basic model has a black rope band and the premium model comes with a link style bracelet which is set with rhinestones. The dial is superb.
Basic model----$125.00 **Premium model-$175.00**

AJ 12 **THE WHOLESALE INTERNET DEALERS LOT. GUARANTEED TO MAKE A PROFIT ! ! !**
This great lot is perfect for resale at shows, markets or through on-line Internet auctions like E-bay or e. Hammer. The items are all very collectible and you can pick out a few pieces to keep and still sell the rest for a sizeable profit ! Believe us, you can't go wrong with this lot -- make extra money from home- the profits are guaranteed and the items are so nice and collectible that they practically sell themselves ! !
The lot includes: two diamond rings from lot 1, the pearl necklace and bracelet set from lot 2, a .20 ct diamond ring from lot 4, five stickpins from lot 5, one diamond stickpin from lot 6, a 20 piece costume jewelry lot, two gents wristwatch from lot 10, and a ladys wristwatch from lot 11. Thirty four pieces in all ! ! ! **$1325.00**

TO ORDER SEND CHECK OR MONEY ORDER TO:

ASHLAND INVESTMENTS
640 SOUTH WASHINGTON BLVD.
SUITE 200
SARASOTA FL. 34236

WATCHES

Watches and jewelry have been closely related from the Georgian era to the present time. Watches reflect the styles and characteristics of the various periods (Victorian, Art Nouveau, Art Deco, etc.) better than many pieces of jewelry!

For example, as the wristwatch evolved, it quickly became the dominant jewelry item for a gentleman of the 1930's, 40's and 50's. Lady's wristwatches were often produced as "miniature jewels" to be worn on the wrist.

Enameled pocketwatches were created as pieces of art as well as timepieces. Craftsmen used pocketwatch cases as canvases to display their artistic engravings and designs.

Since this book is devoted to jewelry, the authors will show pocketwatch and wristwatch examples which have a strong jewelry–related characteristic.

The areas of focus will be enamels, jewel–encrusted cases, form watches and pendants or "lapel watches".

Technical watches or complicated watches such as alarm, chronographs, repeaters, etc., will not be included unless the timepiece also exhibits a strong, jewelry–related value.

The watch collector's field is extremely broad and varied. Readers interested in expanding their knowledge are advised to read the Complete Price Guide to Watches. This annual publication is written by Cooksey Shugart and Richard E. Gilbert.

The primary watch terms used by dealers and collectors will be discussed in the following article.

POCKET AND WRISTWATCHES
AN OVERVIEW OF CASE, DIAL AND MOVEMENT TERMS

A good working knowledge of "the watch vocabulary" is essential when one is appraising, collecting or dealing in timepieces. The three primary elements which make up all watches are the case, movement and dial.

Watch cases were produced in many metals: gold, silver, gold–filled, base metals, etc. As is the case with any fine object, the condition, style and workmanship goes hand in hand with the metal used when judging value.

POCKETWATCHES: CASE TERMS

Hunter case: a case with a lid or cover over the dial. Hunter case consist of a rim, front lid, back lid and an interior dust cover or cuvette.

Open face: a case with an open front over the dial. The dial is protected by a crystal and a bezel.The two most common forms have either a hinged back cover or a "screw back and bezel" design where the parts are threaded and screw on to a central rim.

Demi–hunter: a hunter case with a smaller circle opening in the center of the front lid—this allows a partial view of the interior dial without having to open the lid. Also referred to as a half–hunter.

Pair case: a style commonly used for early verge fusee watches—an interior case holds the movement dial and crystal. This interior case then fits into an outer case which consists of a full back lid and a front bezel.

Swing–out case: a case with an interior ring which holds the movement to the main case. The movement is accessible only when the interior ring is "swung out" from the main case.

Oignon: a French term for very large "onion" cases found on early timepieces from 1725–1780's. These case are generally 55 millimeters in diameter or larger.

Box hinge case: a hunter's case with extended box "frames" near the hinge tubes and/or the upper case area near the pendant.

Biscuit or turnip: both are slang terms used to describe large and heavy cases such as those found on early American keywinds.

Convertible, reversible or Muckle case: unique cases which allow the movement to rotate in such a manner as to change from an open–face style to a hunter style.

WRISTWATCHES: CASE TERMS

The wristwatch case comes in a wide variety of shapes: square, round, rectangle, cushion, oval, tank and tonneau are the primary designs. The majority of wristwatches will be either two or three piece cases. Early cases were often two–piece hinged varieties with wire lugs. Wire lugs refer to a simple bar or tube style end pieces (a ribbon or cloth band could be slipped through). The lugs of a wrist case are the end frames or pieces where a band is attached by the use of a spring bar. Fancy lugs, hooded lugs, moveable or hinged lugs and other unusual styles all enhance the value of a collector's wristwatch.

Wristwatch cases will also be referred to as either snapback or screwback. Generally, the screwback style implies some sort of water–resistant capabilities. Screwback cases generally hold a higher value over a watch where the back simply "snaps on".

WATCH SIZES

Swiss and European pocketwatches are measured in millimeters of the overall case diameter. The movements are measured in lignes. American watches are measured by size (see chart). Sizes 18, 16 and 12 are gents watch sizes and sizes 8, 6, 0 and 3/0 are the standard ladies sizes. The American sizes are measured by the diameter of the watch dial, not the case. Wristwatches are measured in millimeters–the overall diameter of round cases and the length x width for other shapes.

DIALS

Enameled dials were the most popular type for pocketwatches from the 1800's to approximately the 1920s. Then, more cost–efficient metal dials were used. Dial condition and originality is very important to the value of a watch. Hairlines, chips and flakes will diminish the value of an enamel dial.

Early wristwatches (1915–1925) were often produced by fitting a small pocketwatch movement with an enameled dial into a wrist case. As the wristwatch styles changed and movements became thinner in profile, the dials also changed to thinner metal ones. The markers or numerals found on metal dials are either printed or applied (such as "raised" gold numerals). Original dials in good condition will always add a premium to a vintage wristwatch. Refinished dials will lower value since they are not as distinct or precise in the markings.

COMMON DIAL TERMS

Single sunk: refers to an enamel dial with two levels (versus a flat dial). The seconds bit is sunk or recessed to a lower level from the main dial.

Double sunk: a three–piece enamel dial with three levels. The center portion is lower than the outer dial edge and the seconds track is lower than the center.

Seconds track or seconds "bit": the smaller dial (subsidiary dial) which indicates the seconds.

Minute track: the outer ring or marks which indicate the minutes

Montgomery dial: a dial which is marked with individual numerals (1–60) to indicate the minutes.

Digital dial: a dial with open apertures (windows) through which revolving minute and hour discs appear.

Fancy dial: a dial with colorful designs—enamel dials with the colors baked "in" the dial as part of the original process. Hand painted dials will have less value than original fancy dials—also beware of color transfer and decal–enhanced dials.

Mystery dial: a dial which gives the illusion of the hands "floating" on the surface or not connected to the center post of the movement.

WATCH MOVEMENTS

Learning the technical aspects of mechanical watches can seem over-bearing to the beginner. However, the basics are fairly easy to understand.

All mechanical watches are powered by a main spring (this is wound by either a key or by a stem). The power from the mainspring is transferred to a series of gears and pinions (train gears). The applied power must then be released or be allowed to "escape" in a controlled manner. The part of the watch movement which controls this release of power is called the escapement. The primary escapements used in pocketwatches were the verge, cylinder, duplex and lever escapements.

The friction cased by the moving train gears and pinions is reduced by the use of small jewels. The jewels hold oil and therefore reduce wear on the pivots. The most important wheel in a watch movement is the balance wheel—this regulates the release of power in conjunction with the escape-ment.

The gears and pinions of a watch moment are supported by plates or bridges. The plates are referred to as nickel (rhodium plated) or gilt (gold on brass).

Many nickel pocketwatch movements are damascened or decorated with patterns or line designs to add visual interest to the movement. Some movements are also called two–tone for their combination of gold and nick-el finishes.

Mechanical wristwatches are found mainly with lever escapements and the movements are termed manual wind or automatic. A manual wind watch must be wound from the stem or crown while an automatic or "perpetual" wind movement winds the mainspring through the motion of the arm, which then oscillates an interior rotor.

The study of watch mechanisms fills volumes and new collectors should learn as much as possible. Repairs to vintage watches can be very cost-ly. The advice of an expert watchmaker or a reputable dealer should always be sought before determining the value of a non–running watch.

Type: LADIES POCKETWATCHES

General tips on pricing: Prices in this section are for watches that are in reasonably good running order. The prices will also reflect the values for the typical quality which you will find in todays market. The ladies watches are generally found with a fancier style of engraving and the listed prices will reflect this. Watches which are plain in finish will have a much lower value. On the other hand, examples such as high relief gold cases and gold cases with diamonds or gemstones will carry a higher value. Multicolor cases will increase in value with the more multicolor areas they show. The addition of gemstones to watch cases will also add value. Enamel watches will carry a higher value if a matching original pin is included. Enamel on silver watch pins will range in price from $50 to $100 and enamel on gold pins will generally start at $100 and go up depending on the design and number of gemstones. The enamel on watch cases should be in good condition without flakes, chips, scratches, or poor repairs. As a general rule, hunters case watches will be priced higher than open face examples.

Watch abbreviations:

j	the jewels found in the movement
s	the size of the watch (see size chart)
of	openface case
hc	hunters case
gf	gold filled
kwks	a keywind and keyset watch (note: if if no setting is listed

the reader can assume that the watch is a stem wind)

GENERAL PRICING LEVELS----LADYS POCKETWATCHES

gold filled of 0s	35	60	80
gold filled of 6s	35	60	80
silver of 0s	35	60	80
silver of 6s	50	75	85
14k of 0s	65	125	150
14k of 6s	70	125	150
18k of 0s	75	150	200
18k of 6s	100	175	225
gf hc 0s	75	150	200
gf hc 6s	60	130	185
silver hc 0s	60	130	175
silver hc 6s	60	130	175
14k hc 0s	200	350	400
14k hc 6s	200	325	375
18k hc 0s	225	375	500
18k hc 6s	250	375	500
multicolor 0s gf of	100	175	200
multicolor 6s gf of	100	175	200
multicolor 0s silver of	75	125	175
multicolor 6s silver of	75	125	175
multicolor 14k 0s of	200	350	450
multicolor 14k 6s of	200	350	450
multicolor 0s gf hc	150	300	350
multicolor 6s gf hc	150	300	350
multicolor 0s silver hc	150	275	350
multicolor 6s silver hc	150	275	350
multicolor 14k 0s hc	400	600	750
multicolor 14k 6s hc	400	600	750
enamel on gf of	150	300	400
enamel on gf hc	200	400	500
enamel on silver of	150	300	400
enamel on silver hc	200	400	500
enamel on 14k of	400	700	900
enamel on 14k hc	500	900	1200

SLIDE CHAINS

Slide chains were very popular from the1860's to the 1920's. They are normally at least 48 inches long with a swivel end and a slide. The chain is doubled around the neck and the doubled strand is placed through the swivel. The watch bow is also placed in the swivel and the chain now forms a double "V" pattern with the slide being in the middle. The length can be adjusted by moving the slide. Values of slide chains are determined by the metal, link design, and the condition. Slides will vary from the plain to very ornate and fancier types will command a premium. Gold filled slide chains with simple gold slides will sell for $75 to $100. Fancy link styles and chains with very ornate slides will be priced higher. Gold slide chains will range from around $400 for the lighter and simpler styles. Fancy link and heavier chains will bring higher prices. Chains with gemstone ornamented slides or fine stone cameo slides are very strong and they can range from $1000 and up.

Type: LADIES WRISTWATCHES

General tips on pricing: Generally speaking, ladies wristwatches are not collectible unless the cases are either gold or platinum. Even in gold, the very plain style watches are often not restored and they will only bring a small dollar amount for the gold bullion value of the case. A typical small ladies wristwatch case will have a gold weight of three or four dwts. (approx $20 to $30 in todays gold market for 14k gold). Jewelry and watch buyers are interested in watches with a good jewelry "look", gemstone ornamentation, enameling, or a nicely designed gold bracelet.   Watches should be in good running order and the dials should be clean in appearance and not spotted. The "base" price of many watches in this category will be the gold or platinum value plus the value of the gemstones. Added to this base value is the premium the watch will bring due to styling and design. By reviewing the various examples the reader will become more familiar with the price levels of jewelry related wristwatches. When purchasing a gold bracelet watch, it is important that the length of the bracelet is correct for your wrist size. Shortening a bracelet is normally not a problem but adding length can be difficult depending on the complexity of the link design. Watches produced by the more prestigious manufacterers will bring a premium over those made by the larger producers.

GENERAL PRICING LEVELS--LADIES WRISTWATCHES
(note: prices are for restored watches in running order)

14k case no gemstones	30	60	80
18k case no gemstones	45	70	90
platinum case no gemstones	75	125	175
gold case with .25 ct tw diamonds	100	150	175
platinum case .25 ct tw diamonds	150	200	225
gold case with .50 ct tw diamonds	150	250	300
platinum case .50 ct tw diamonds	200	400	500
gold case with 1.00 ct tw diamonds	400	600	800
platinum with 1.00 ct tw diamonds	450	700	850
gold case with 2.00 ct tw diamonds	600	1200	1400
platinum case 2.00 ct tw diamonds	750	1500	1800
enameled bezel, silver case	100	200	250
enameled bezel, gold case	150	300	400
14k bracelet ww 10 dwts	100	200	250
18k bracelet ww 10 dwts	150	250	300
14k bracelet ww 20 dwts	200	400	500
18k bracelet ww 20 dwts	300	500	600
14k bracelet ww 20 dwts and .50 ct tw dia	300	550	700
18k bracelet ww 20 dwts and .50 ct tw dia	425	700	800
platinum bracelet 20 dwts and .50 ct tw dia	550	850	1000
14k bracelet ww 20 dwts 1.00 ct tw diamonds	600	900	1000
18k bracelet ww 20 dwts 1.00 ct tw diamonds	700	1000	1200
platinum bracelet 20 dwts 1.00 ct tw diamonds	800	1200	1400
14k rose with rubies and diamonds (tw .20 ct)	125	200	250
14k rose with rubies and diamonds (tw .50 ct)	200	300	400
14k rose with rubies and diamonds (tw 1.00 ct)	400	600	700
Ring watch 14k open dial	200	350	450
Ring watch 14k covered dial	250	400	500

MENS POCKET WATCHES AND WRISTWATCHES

Gents' pocket and vintage wristwatches are extremely collectible items. The relationship to the jewelry market however is fairly limited. Most of the collectors pocket watches are valued based on mechanical features, rarity, case style and other technical aspects. Mens wristwatches are evaluated along similar lines. The use of gemstones with gents watches can be found on diamond dial watches, some cases which are set with diamonds or sapphires, and diamond bezel pieces. Enamel was also used for decorating wrist and pocket watch bezels. Colorful examples from the Art Deco period are especially desireable. Readers who are interested in learning more about pocket and wristwatches should refer to "The Complete Price Guide To Watches". This book is an annual publication with a wealth of information about every phase of the watch market. The authors are Cooksey Shugart and Richard Gilbert. The book is published by Cooksey Shugart Publications P.O. Box 3147 Cleveland Tn. 37320-3147.

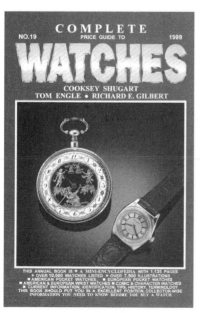

If you would like a copy of The Complete Price Guide To Watches send check or money order to

**Ashland Investments
640 S. Washington Blvd.
Suite 200
Sarasota Fl. 34236**

Over 10,000 watches listed and 7,500 illustrations. Current information, identification,tips,history and terminology

26.95 plus $ 6.00 shipping
in the United States.

LADYS POCKET WATCHES
DIAMOND AND FANCY GOLD

Swiss 18k hc, with flower
pin, sm diamonds on case,
30 mm c.1920
300 450 600

Swiss 18k, hc, 24 mm with
Art Nouveau floral motif, ribbon bow pin
c.1910
500 700 900 ☆

14k hc with two sm
diamonds, round
emerald, Swiss, 27
mm
c.1915
250 350 450

18k hc with five rose cut
diamonds, Swiss, 28 mm
c.1910
250 350 450

LADYS POCKET WATCHES
DIAMOND AND FANCY GOLD

18k hc with 12 rose cut diamonds on case, 9 dia-
monds on the bar pin (tw
.20 ct), Swiss 26 mm
c. 1915
350 550 650

18k hc with diamonds 26
mm, Swiss, with star form
14k pin set with half pearls
and sm diamond
c.1910
500 700 800 ☆

18k multicolor hc, Swiss, 25
mm, rose green and yellow
gold flowers in raised relief
c.1910
400 600 700 ☆

Tiffany platinum watch, sm
diamonds and onyx on
bezel, ribbon bow pin with
sm diamonds, 24 mm,
Swiss, c.1910
700 1200 1500 ☆

LADYS POCKET WATCHES
DIAMOND AND FANCY GOLD

18k of Swiss with sm
rubies and diamonds
Art Nouveau motif
matching pin, c.1920
400 750 900 ☆

Swiss 18k, 26 mm,
of, fancy case with
sm diamonds, scal-
loped rim matching
gold bow pin c.1905
400 750 900 ☆

Swiss 18k with half
pearls, matching pin,
27mm, of, c.1900
800 1400 1800 ☆ ☆

Waltham high relief Griffin
design, 18k of, 21 mm, with
matching pin, c.1905
850 1500 1800 ☆ ☆

LADYS POCKET WATCHES
DIAMOND AND FANCY GOLD

Swiss 18k of, 26 mm, case and pin set with diamonds (tw .70 ct) high relief swirl motif, c.1905
1200 2000 2500 ☆☆

Platinum pendant watch, Swiss, of, with sm diamond garland motif, 24 mm, matching 26" chain set with pearl spacers, 21 dwts Edwardian, c.1905
1500 2500 3000 ☆☆

LADYS POCKET WATCHES
ENAMEL ON SILVER

Swiss 30 mm, of, blue and gold enamel on sterling, ribbon pin, c.1900
200 350 450

New England watch co. 32 mm, of, enamel on silver, fleur de lis pin c.1900
200 350 450

Swiss 30mm, of, black lavender,and green enamel on .800 fine silver, Art Nouveau c.1920
250 400 500 ☆

Swiss ball shaped watch, enamel on silver, 23 mm, of, with matching chain c.1930
200 400 500

LADYS POCKET WATCHES
ENAMEL ON SILVER

Swiss 30 mm, of, .800 silver with blue and gold enamel, outer half pearl bezels c.1900
200 400 500 ☆

Swiss, 22x30 mm, of, enamel on silver, colorful flowers, matching chain c.1920
225 450 550 ☆

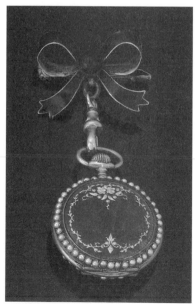

Swiss, 30 mm enamel on silver, of, pearl outer border, matching pin c. 1900
225 450 550 ☆

Swiss portrait enamel, of, 30 mm, sterling, finely detailed poly-chrome scene, matching pin, c.1900
300 600 800 ☆

LADYS POCKET WATCHES
ENAMEL ON GOLD

Swiss guilloche enamel, 18k, of, 22 mm, sm diamond in wg filigree central frame, 14k neck chain c.1920
400 650 800 ☆

Swiss keywind, 18k hc, 41 mm, blue, black and white enamel c.1875
400 750 900

Le Coultre 18k, 28 mm, of, with enamel and central diamond, circle pin with pearls and enamel.
c.1915
500 1000 1200 ☆☆

LADYS POCKET WATCHES
ENAMEL ON GOLD

Swiss 18k hc, 30 mm,
red enamel flower on
front, plain back,
c.1900
350 700 900

Swiss 18k hc, 41 mm, keywind with
black Victorian enamel, 14k slide
chain, 60 ", with enameled slide
c.1875 (note: see slide chain examples at the end of this section)
800 1500 2000 ☆☆

Swiss 18k hc, 28 mm, enameled scenes on both sides,
c.1895
450 800 900 ☆

Swiss 18k of,
enameled back
with polychrome
floral design, 30
mm,
c.1875
400 600 800 ☆

LADYS POCKET WATCHES
ENAMEL ON GOLD

Swiss 18k hc, plain
front, enameled por-
trait with sm rose dia-
mond ornaments, 25
mm, c.1900
500 900 1200 ☆

Swiss 18k hc, 31 mm,
sm rose cut diamonds
and enameled flower
motif on front , leaf pattern on back, c.1905
500 850 1000 ☆

Swiss 18k, of, 25 mm, fine
enameled copper leaves, black
background, upper diamond
area, enamel pin with diamond
and pearl c.1910
600 1000 1200 ☆

Swiss 18k, hc, 24mm, guilloche cherry red enamel on
both sides, nine rose cut
diamonds, enameled ribbon
bow pin,
c.1905
800 1500 1800 ☆

LADYS POCKET WATCHES
ENAMEL ON GOLD

Swiss 18k, of, 25 mm,
sm rose diamonds,
red enamel, engraved
gold leaves, fleur-de-
lis pin, c.1905
500 800 1000 ☆ ·

SLIDE CHAINS

Slide chains were very popular from the 1860's to the 1920's. They are normally at least 48 inches long with a swivel end and a slide. The chain is doubled around the neck and the doubled strand is placed through the swivel. The watch bow is also placed in the swivel and the chain now forms a double "V" pattern with the slide being in the middle. The length can be adjusted by moving the slide. Values of slide chains are determined by the metal, link design, and the condition. Slides will vary from the plain to very ornate - fancier types will command a premium. Gold filled slide chains with simple gold slides will sell for $75 to $100. Fancy link styles and chains with very ornate slides will be priced higher. Gold slide chains will range from around $400 for the lighter and simpler styles. Fancy link and heavier chains will bring higher prices. Chains with gemstone ornamented slides or fine stone cameo slides are very strong and they can range from $1000 and up.

Slide chain, 14k fancy link, 70", 18k flower slide set with diamonds (tw.50 ct) sm rubies and sapphires, 36 dwts, c.1915
800 1500 2000

Slide chain , 14k fancy link , 60 ", 20x25 mm Art Nouveau flower slide with pearl, 39 dwts c.1900
800 1500 1700

Victorian slide chain, 14k, 54", 15 dwts, gold slide with small stone cameo c.1880
300 500 600

LADYS ENAMEL AND
EARLY WRISTWATCHES

Swiss enamel on bezel
and back, coin silver, 28
mm, with early fancy gf
band, c.1920
150 300 400

Swiss 18k, 14x21
mm, light and dark
blue enamel on
bezel Art Deco,
c. 1930
175 350 450 ☆

Swiss 18k, 14x21 mm,
red, black and blue
enamel, c.1930
250 425 500 ☆

Swiss 18k 24 mm, black
enamel line patterns,
four sm diamonds
c.1910
250 450 550

Ballerina watch pin,
1-1/2 long, 18k yel-
low and wg, Swiss
c.1930
200 400 500

Swiss 18k, 14x21
mm, Art Deco with
blue, red, green
and black
enamel c.1930
300 600 750 ☆

Early ww, Swiss,
18k 25 mm.with
eight sm diamonds
(tw .30 ct)
c.1915
200 350 425 ☆

LADYS ENAMEL AND
EARLY WRISTWATCHES

Swiss signed "Tiffany", 18k,
25 mm, ten sm single cut
diamonds c.1915
200 400 500

Swiss octagon 18k, 22 mm,
eight diamonds (tw .30 ct) with
gf band
c. 1920
200 400 500

Juvenia (Swiss) plat-
inum 20 mm, with sm
diamonds (tw .15 ct)
c. 1910
200 350 500

Swiss 18k, 25mm,
fancy scroll design
ends with sm dia-
monds, sm sap-
phires,
c.1910
300 550 650 ☆

Rare enamel and gold pocketwatches c. 1885-1915

Magnificent jewel set pocketwatches c. 1895-1920

A collection of antique wristwatches c. 1920-1950

Rare Victorian enameled bracelet watches, an exquisite French enameled box, unusual enamel and gold ring watch

LADYS ENAMEL AND
EARLY WRISTWATCHES

Swiss 18k, 24 mm,
white and blue enamel
trim, eight sm diamonds
(tw .25 ct) 18k expan-
sion band
c.1920
400 700 850

Swiss early ww with diamonds
18k, 25 mm, 18k band, full
diamond bezel with tw .65 ct.
c.1915
500 900 1100 ☆

LADYS DIAMOND WRISTWATCHES

Swiss, plat, 14x24
mm, sm sapphires,
28 sm diamonds
(tw.65 ct) wg rope
band,
 c.1920
300 500 600

Hamilton, 14k wg.
18 mm. diamonds
on lugs and band,
(tw .53 ct) 12 dwts
c.1940
350 650 750

Swiss, platinum,
12x20 mm, 12
diamonds on
case, diamond
links (tw .75 ct)
c.1925
400 800 950

Swiss 18k wg,
14x32 mm, dial
signed Tiffany, 32
diamonds (tw .80
ct) c. 1930
375 750 900

Swiss platinum,
10x26 mm, fifty
round diamonds
(tw .75 ct)
c. 1920
450 900 1100

LADYS DIAMOND WRISTWATCHES

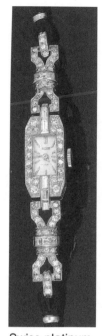

Hamilton, platinum,
14x18 mm, round
and baguette dia-
monds, (tw 1.85 ct)
14k wg band
c. 1930
500 1000 1200

Swiss platinum,
10x23 mm, fancy
diamond links
and bezel,
(tw 2.10 ct)
c. 1930
750 1500 2000 ☆☆

Swiss platinum, 10x27
mm, case is set with
100 diamonds
(tw 2.00 ct) c. 1920
1000 2000 2500 ☆☆

Paul Ditisheim (high
grade Swiss) 14k wg,
14x49 mm, calibre cut
sapphires, numerous
diamonds (tw 2.00 ct)
c. 1920
1100 2200 2700 ☆☆

Patek Philippe, plat-
inum, 19x25 mm, eigh-
teen jewel, high grade,
diamond bezel and
covered ends (tw 1.00
ct) c. 1920
1250 2500 3000 ☆☆

LADYS DIAMOND WRISTWATCHES

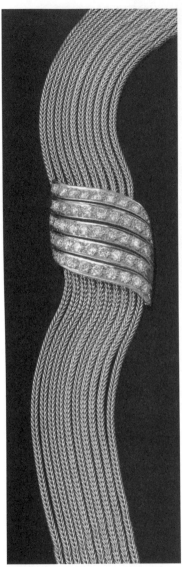

Gold and diamond covered dial,
14k ten strand bracelet, wg swirl
top cover with 2.50 ct tw diamonds, 32 dwts Swiss
c. 1940
1250 2500 3000 ☆

Blancpain (Swiss)
bracelet ww, 18k cuff
style with platinum and
diamond top (tw .75 ct),
14 mm wide, 18 dwts,
c. 1940
1500 2750 3250 ☆·

LADYS DIAMOND WRISTWATCHES

Hamilton, platinum, 18mm, double link band with diamonds, round and baguette diamonds on case (tw 4.75 ct) c. 1940
1500 3000 3500 ☆☆

Retro period covered dial, 15x36 mm case with 42 diamonds (tw 1.71 ct), platinum with brick link band, 35 dwts, high grade Swiss Audemars Piguet c. 1940
1500 3000 3500 ☆☆

LADY'S GOLD BRACELET WATCHES

Swiss, 18k , 16 mm,
link bracelet, 20 dwts
c. 1930
200 400 500

Swiss 18k , fancy
bracelet, 18 mm
wide, 16 dwts,
c. 1940
200 400 500

Cyma (Swiss)18k,
fancy 11 mm wide
band, 25 dwts
c. 1930
225 425 525

Swiss rose gold,
14k, 14 mm, sm
diamonds, six
rubies, 12 dwts
c. 1940
225 425 525

Hamilton, 14k
rose gold, 12 sm
diamonds (tw .24
ct) calibre cut
rubies, 8 dwts,
21x37 mm,
c. 1940
225 425 525 ☆

LADY'S GOLD BRACELET WATCHES

Swiss 18k, fancy
bracelet ww, 19 mm,
sm diamonds on
bezel (tw .30 ct) 17
dwts
c. 1930
250 500 600

Swiss 18k, 20 mm wide
four section bracelet,
four rectangular rubies,
sm diamonds (tw .16 ct)
19 dwts
c. 1930
250 500 600

Swiss 18k fancy
bracelet, 14 mm
case, 24 dwts
c. 1940
250 500 600

Swiss 14k, cov-
ered dial, six
opals, three sm
diamonds,15 mm
diameter, 17 dwts
c. 1950
300 550 650

Swiss 18k ww, 16mm
wide, fancy bracelet,
dial signed "Tiffany"
Movado movement,
18 dwts,
c. 1935
300 600 700

LADY'S GOLD BRACELET WATCHES

Swiss 18k floral
band , 15mm
wide case with
rubies and dia-
monds (tw .18 ct)
17.5 dwts
c. 1930
300 600 700 ☆

Le Coultre (Swiss)
14k yellow and white,
unusual band, 15x18
mm case, 12.5 dwts
c. 1940
350 650 750 ☆

Swiss cover dial ww,
14k, 19 mm " fold
over " dial cover, sm
diamond accent,
20 dwts c. 1940
300 600 700

Rolex 18k, 15 mm
round case, 17j man-
ual wind, two .08 ct
diamonds 12 dwts
c. 1950
375 750 850

LADY'S GOLD BRACELET WATCHES

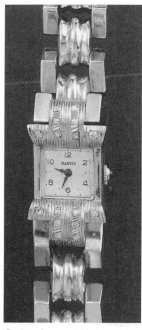

Swiss 18k rose gold,
square rubies, round
diamonds (tw .36 ct)
27 dwts Retro
c. 1940
350 700 800 ☆

Swiss fancy 18k bracelet
ww, 17mm wide, dia-
monds in platinum
(tw .40 ct) 30 dwts,
c.1930
350 700 800

Swiss 14x22mm case,
18k rose, twenty round
rubies, eight diamonds
(tw .16 ct) 14 dwts
c. 1930
475 950 1100 ☆

Omega covered dial,
18k, seven diamonds
(tw .16ct) 16 mm
diameter, 24 dwts
c. 1950
450 900 1000

Swiss 14k bracelet ww,
twenty diamonds (tw
1.00 ct), 24 rubies
(tw 1.00 ct) 22 mm
diameter, c. 1950
600 1200 1400

Omega 18k bracelet ww,
fancy leaf design, hinged
bracelet, 15 mm case, 30
dwts, c.1950
400 800 900

LADY'S GOLD BRACELET WATCHES

Swiss unusual "pineapple" leaf covered dial ww, heavy 18k , finely detailed leaf links, diamonds in wg mounts on top (tw .70 ct) 20 mm across, c. 1940
650 1300 1500 ☆

MISCELLANEOUS

Box with shell cameo, 2-1/2" x 1-1/2", granite with
fine shell cameo St George motif,
   c. 1870   300 600 700

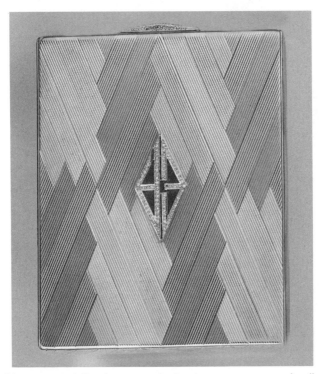

Gold compact, 14k criss cross design in rose, green and yellow
gold,   4"x3" numerous sm diamonds at center and on clasp,
signed   "Videll and Ballow "   100 dwts c.1920
750   1500   1800

MISCELLANEOUS

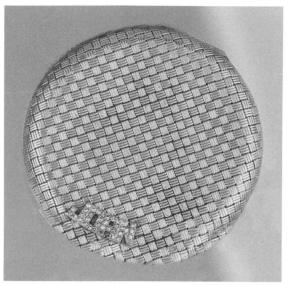

Gold compact,signed "Tiffany", 14k, 3" diameter, 64 dwts, 36 diamonds form name plate (.36 ct tw)
c. 1930   500 1000 1200

Musical charm 21x27 mm, 14k, fancy engraved
c. 1920
175 350 450

Gold hairpins, 18k with Lapis lazuli and sm pearl ends, 60 mm long c. 1915
150 300 400

MISCELLANEOUS

Rosary 18k with black
onyx beads, 22", finely
detailed 18k cross
gold links
c. 1930
125 250 325

Musical charm 20x25 mm,
14k, 11 dwts sm ruby and
sapphire c. 1920
175 350 450

MISCELLANEOUS

Rosary ,18k links, mother-of-pearl
beads, 30", Victorian gold cross
and center frame
c. 1895
250 500 600

Rosary, 14k, 28" gold links
and cross, coral beads
c. 1910
175 350 450

MISCELLANEOUS

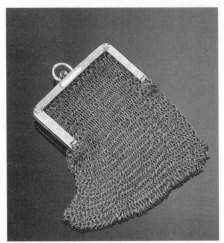

Gold purse 14k, 30x56 mm, 10 dwts
c. 1920
100 200 250

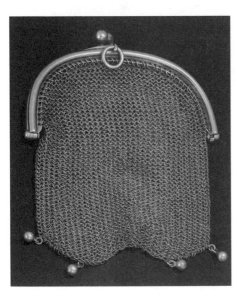

Gold purse 14k, 2-1/2"
curved top frame, gold
ball dangles
28 dwts c. 1920
275 550 650

MISCELLANEOUS

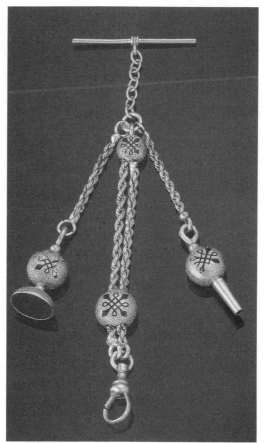

Gold Chatelaine, 14k with black enamel accents,
T-bar, winding key, swivel, initial seal fob, 4" long,
9 dwts c. 1870
275 550 650

MISCELLANEOUS

Victorian watch chain, 18k, 15 dwts, 9" long, central slide, swivel, swing ring, tassel fobs
c. 1870
200 400 500

Gold watch chain, 18k ,10" long, 15 dwts, T-bar, swivel, ball shaped slide, bloodstone seal fob,
c. 1880
250 500 600

ANTIQUE JEWELRY
Outstanding values
on fine estate jewelry.

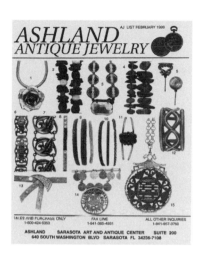

ASHLAND OFFERS AN EVERY OTHER MONTH BLACK AND WHITE LIST WITH A COLOR INSERT. CONTAINING 200 PIECES OF ESTATE AND ANTIQUE JEWELRY, WITH AN EXCITING AUCTION STYLE BID SHEET FOR ITEMS THAT DO NOT SELL AT LIST PRICE

The Ashland color catalog series includes some of the finest antique jewelry ever made, at the best prices.It is a must for the avid collector and fine jewelry lover.

If you would like to recieve these catalogs
free of charge call or write to:

ASHLAND
INVESTMENTS
640 S. WASHINGTON BLVD.
SUITE 200
SARASOTA FL. 34236
(941) 957-3760 1-800-424-5353

ADAMANTINE

Taken from the Greek word for diamond "adamas", this word refers to the brilliant surface luster of a diamond.

AIGRETTE

A spray of gems set in a flower form or as a feather motif. Usually worn in the hair or on a hat.

ARABESQUES

A style of scroll work, small ornate swirl patterns or engravings.

BAKELITE

A synthetic resin (phenol formaldehyde) used in interesting, low–priced jewelry during the 1930's. Popular for colorful bracelets, large pins and necklaces.

BANGLE

A bracelet which is hinged to form two halves. Also used to describe a thin, round bracelet which slips over the hand.

BAGUETTE

A narrow, rectangular cut stone (i.e. diamond baguette). The term is also used to describe slender, rectangular ladies wristwatches of the 1930's.

BAROQUE

A term for large irregularly–shaped pearls. Also used to describe highly ornate engravings or designs.

BASE METAL

Used to describe a variety of non–precious metals (brass, etc.)

BASSETAILLE

An enamel technique consisting of transparent enamel over an engraved or "patterned" metal ground.

BEZEL

A recessed groove or flange used to secure a stone. In watches, the ring which holds a watch crystal in place.

BOG OAK

A peat–like material or darkened oak wood. Popular for carved jewelry of Irish origin during the Victorian era.

BRILLIANT

A standard cut for diamonds, with fifty–eight facets. Named for its superior brilliant refraction qualities.

BRIOLETTE

A faceted gem in a teardrop or pear shape.

BROOCH

A term used for pins; usually the larger–sized pieces (cameos, etc.), from the French "broche".

CABOCHON

A stone which is cut so the top forms a curved convex surface.

CAMEO

A two or three layer stone which is carved in relief

CARAT

A standard weight for precious gems. The metric carat equals one–fifth of a gram. One ounce avoirdupois equals 141.75 carats.

CASTING

A process using a mold and the "lost wax" method to form rings, mounts and other jewelry pieces.

CHATOYANCY

A silky band of light or reflections which form a "cat's eye" effect on cabochon cut stones.

CHAMPLEVE

An enamel technique; enamel is placed in shallow cut–outs which are engraved in a metal ground.

CHANNEL SET

A style of stone setting where the outer sides of the mount hold the stone in place. Stones are set close together to form a straight line.

CHATELAINE

A decorative hook or clasp with several chains. Used to hold thimbles, scissors, keys. A functional accessory which became ornate and decorative in the 17th century.

CHOKER

A short necklace or strand of beads, usually fifteen inches long.

CLOISONNE

From the French "cloisons", metal cells are set on a base and then filled with enamel flux.

COIN SILVER

An alloy used for U.S. silver coins, watch cases, etc. Coin silver is 900/1000 (90%) fine silver with the balance copper.

COLLET

A setting consisting of a curved metal band or "strip" which holds a gem in place. Similar to a bezel style setting.

CUFF BRACELET

Term used to describe wider bracelets with an open back. Also referred to as "slave bracelets".

CULET

The bottom facet of a brilliant or European cut diamond.

DAMASKEENED

The decorative art of producing designs or patterns on metal. Often used to ornament watch movements. A technique of gold and silver inlays set in iron or steel.

DEPOSE

French—a patent or copyright stamp found on jewelry.

DOG COLLAR

A wide necklace or band worn tight around the neck. Composed of several strands (pearls, beads, etc.) Or a broad ribbon with gems.

DOUBLETS

A composite stone made from a genuine stone which is joined to glass or other materials.

DROP

A small ornament or gem suspended from a chain. Also refers to a style of long earrings.

ELECTROPLATE

An electromagnetic plating process which deposits fine gold (or silver or rhodium) onto a less valuable material such as brass or base metal.

255

ENAMEL
>A decorative technique using colored glass or glaze which is fused onto a metal base.

EPNS
>An abbreviation for electroplated nickel silver, a silver plate tech nique.

ETRUSCAN
>A 19th Century antique revival period based on the early works of the ancient Etruscans in the 6th and 7th centuries. Granulation designs were used extensively in this style.

FACET
>A small plane or flat surface cut into a stone to enhance the refraction of light.

FILIGREE
>Metalwork forming lacy patterns and delicate designs. Platinum and gold filigree work was often used to form ring mounts and fancy pin frames.

FINDINGS
>The "finishing" or connecting parts used in jewelry making—catches, clasps, springrings, swivels, jump rings, etc.

FIRE
>The brilliancy of gems or the degree of dispersion of light as it relates to diamonds, opals, etc.

FLEUR DE LIS
>French for "flower of light" a symbol designed from the iris flower—often found on Victorian and Edwardian jewelry pieces.

GERMAN SILVER
>An alloy of nickel, zinc and copper; also known as nickel silver. There is no silver content.

GIRDLE
>The outer edge of a faceted or brilliant–cut diamond

GOLD FILLED
>A composite made from joining a layer or layers of gold alloy to a base metal alloy.

GRANULATION

Delicate and small beads of gold or other metal used as a surface decoration. Primarily used during the Etruscan period.

GRISAILLE

A painted enamel technique which produces a light and shade effect through the use of an engraved background, an opaque white undercoat and a transparent surface enamel.

GUILLOCHE

An enamel effect created by a translucent polychrome enamel placed over an engraved geometric design.

GUTTA PERCHA

A dark brown substance produced from the Malayan palaquilon tree. Used in jewelry production and for photo frame covers in the 1800's.

HARDNESS

The resistance a mineral has to abrasions or scratches (refer to Moh's scale).

INCLUSIONS

Natural particles or foreign matter which are enclosed within a gemstone.

INTAGLIO

To carve or cut a design into a gem or other type material (unlike a cameo which is carved in a raised pattern).

IRIDESCENT

A high luster formed on pearls or a prism–like play of colors on a gemstone.

KARAT

A standard measure of fineness used for gold. 24 Karat is fine gold. One karat equals 1/24. 14 Karat gold is 14/24 fine gold and the balance (10/24) is alloy.

LAVALIERE

A jewelry ornament or drop suspended from a chain which is worn around the neck. Named for Louise de la Valliere, a mistress of Louis XIV.

LOCKET
A closed pendant made to hold a small photo or lock of hair.

LORGNETTE
An opera glass or pair of eyeglasses usually attached to a handle. Some were designed to fold in half. Many had fancy engraved or jewel encrusted handles and frames.

LOUPE
A small hand–held magnifier (usually 10 power) used for examining gemstones and jewelry.

LUSTER
The effect produced by light reflected from the surface of a stone or pearl.

MATINEE
Used as a term to describe pearls or other necklaces with a length of approx. 24–26 inches.

MELEE
Small diamonds ranging in size from .01 ct to .10 ct

MILLEFIORI
A term used to describe multi–colored glass beads used to create small colorful miniatures which are known as mosaics.

MOHS SCALE
A scale of hardness used by mineralogists. Created by Frederick Mohs, the scale denotes an order of hardness with the diamond being the "hardest".

MOTHER OF PEARL
The iridescent "interior" shell layer from a pearl oyster.

MOUNT
The setting or frame which holds a gemstone in place

NACRE
A substance which forms the lining of many shells—pearls are formed from layers of nacre.

NICKEL SILVER
A composition with no silver—an alloy of nickel, copper and zinc.

NIELLO
An enamel technique which produces a rick black color—this is usually recessed and forms and outline or shadow around a gold or silver design.

OPACITY
Lacking transparency, impervious to light

OPERA
As in "opera length", a longer strand of pearls—more than 30 inches in length

ORIENT
A term used to describe the sheen or iridescent "play" exhibited by a pearl

PARURE
A matching set of jewelry—a set can consist of a necklace, earrings, bracelet and a pin or ring. "Demi–parure" refers to a partial set.

PASTE
An imitation stone made from leaded glass. The term is used to describe many varieties of glass–like imitation stones.

PAVE
As in pave settings—a style of gem setting where stones are set very close together with a minimal amount of metal showing between them.

PAVILION
The lower portion of a diamond below the girdle

PENNYWEIGHT
The term was originally the weight of an Anglo–Norman penny. Now used to mean one twentieth of a troy ounce. The term is abbreviated as dwt.

PINCHBECK
Introduced in the 1700's, this process was an early "imitation" gold invented by London clockmaker Christopher Pinchbeck. The process combined brass and zinc to form a gold–colored metal.

PIQUE

Decorative silver or gold appliques which were pinned trough tor toiseshell or painted horn cases on watches in the 1725–1820 time frame.

PLIQUE A JOUR

An enamel technique where openwork frames are filled with translucent enamel to form a "stained glass" effect.

REPOUSSE

Decorative work—metal is pressed or hammered from the back so that the design appears in raised relief on the front of the object.

RHODIUM

A white metal element derived from platinum, used for electro-plating.

ROCK CRYSTAL

A clear quartz sometimes cut and used as a "frosted" center piece for antiquebrooches or pins. Also used as a crystal on some antique watches.

ROLLED GOLD

A process similar to gold–filled but generally made from a thinner layer of gold.

RONDELLES

Gold or other metal beads used as spacers on necklaces and bracelets.

ROSE CUT

An early diamond cut with fewer facets than later brilliant cuts

SAUTOIR

A very long necklace or chain with bead or stone ornaments spaced at regular intervals. Often with a central slide or tassels.

SILK

Fibers or rod–like inclusions seen in rubies and emeralds which exhibit a "silky" sheen

SILVER GILT

Silver with a light coating of gold or a golden lacquer

STERLING
> .925 fine— a fixed proportion of 925% fine silver and 75% copper

SYNTHETIC
> Manufactured stones which have a similar structure and composition as the natural minerals they imitate

TABLE
> The top flat facet of a brilliant–cut diamond

TRANSLUCENT
> Partially transparent—some light is transmitted but no clear outlines will be seen through a translucent stone

TRANSPARENT
> A stone is transparent if objects can be clearly seen through it

TREMBLANT
> A type of setting where gems are set on hidden springs which allows them to quiver and therefore exhibit more "sparkle"

VERMEIL
> A term for silver gilt or gold plate on silver

VITREOUS
> A glassy look or a luster which resembles glass